NO OTHER WAY

Jack Russia
and the Spanish Civil War

A Biography

by

RICHARD FELSTEAD

ALUN BOOKS

3 Crown Street, Port Talbot, West Glamorgan

© Richard Felstead, 1981

ISBN 0 907117 05 8 (Hardback) £4·95

ISBN 0 907117 00 7 (Paperback) £2·95

946·081

F3(12)

£4.95

Acknowledgements are due to the following for permission to use copyright material : to Hamish Hamilton Ltd. for the quotation from **Days of Hope** by André Malraux ; to the Author's Literary Estate and Chatto & Windus Ltd. for extracts from ' Benicasim ' by Sylvia Townsend Warner ; to Faber & Faber Ltd. for an extract from ' Spain 1937 ' from **The English Auden : Poems, Essays and Dramatic Writings 1927–1939 ;** to the Executors of the Estate of C. Day Lewis, Jonathan Cape Ltd. and the Hogarth Press for an extract from ' The Volunteer ' from **Collected Poems.** 1954 ; to the Hogarth Press for ' A Moment of War ' from **The Sun My Monument** by Laurie Lee ; to Mr. Eben Morris for extracts from **The Angry Summer** by Idris Davies ; and to Anthony Conran for ' Guernica ' from **Collected Poems.**

Every effort has been made to trace authors and owners of copyrights ; however we would be grateful to hear from any author or copyright holder not acknowledged, so that the omission can be put right.

Printed by Bridgend Printing Co. Ltd., Tremains Road, Bridgend, Mid Glamorgan

CONTENTS

Preface and Acknowledgements

For Dewi and Rhian who have so much, hoping that you will remember your fathers, who had so little.

Also in memory of Robert, a ray of sunshine, who came and went.

> " Your fathers fought and suffered
> And died for their daily bread,
> And on the sides of your mountains
> Sleep the heroic dead.
>
> Bugles will not wake them
> From the eternal night,
> But you will be sons of theirs,
> Keeping their torches bright."

> *Idris Davies* (' The Angry Summer ').

Preface and Acknowledgements

" You are history. You are legend."

La Pasionara.

For many years I have nursed the ambition to tell the story of John Roberts, my grandfather. It is a tale that begs to be told.

I am no historian. Neither am I a writer. There are many others who could better do justice to a worthy life and cause. If this work has any merit, it is the filial pride which inspired it.

I have a double regret in completing this biography. Both my grandfather and Mr. John Williams, the friend who encouraged me to begin the task, are unable to give me their valued opinions. Thirty years separated them in life ; three short months in death. This book was originally intended to be an eightieth birthday present for my grandfather. It now becomes a posthumous tribute.

My tribute could not have been completed without much help and I wish to thank and admit an unpayable debt to Mr. Leo Price, Mr. Lance Rogers, Mr. Alun Menai Williams, Mr. and Mrs. Goff Price, Mr. George Thomas and Mrs. Anne Winnick. I would also like to say a special thank-you to Dr. Hywel Francis of the South Wales Miners' Library, Swansea, for his ready help on many occasions. Quotations from the letters of Frank Owen, Tom Picton and Jim Brewer come from Dr. Francis' Ph.D. thesis " The South Wales Miners and the Spanish Civil War : a study in internationalism." My thanks are also due to my good friend Mr. John Jones for his illustrations, and to my wife Sandra for her illustration and continued interest. I wish to record my debt to Mrs. Pauline Morgan for reading the original script and for her many useful suggestions. To Mrs. Margaret Halpin I am grateful for forfeiting many a lunchtime to type the manuscript.

Finally, I wish to acknowledge the aid given to me by the following people and agencies :

Martin Bobker.
Syd Booth.
Edmund Frow, The Working Class Movement, Manchester.
Harry Gaze.
Nan Green, International Brigade Association.
Tom Hyndman.

Tom Jones.
Maurice Levine.
Joe Norman.
Bernie Rothman.
Philip Toynbee.
Sam Wild.
Bill Williams, Manchester Polytechnic.
Communist Party of Great Britain.
Morning Star.
Rhymney Valley Express.
Western Mail.
World Records (E.M.I.).
Glamorgan Record Office, Cardiff.
South Wales Miners' Library, Swansea.
British Library, London.
Central Library, Shepherd's Bush Road, London.
Southall Library, London.
New York Public Library.
Foreign and Commonwealth Office, London.
British Consulate General, Marseilles.
Mairie d'Arles, Bouches-du-Rhone, France.
French Government Tourist Office.
Ministerio de Comercio y Turismo, Spain.

Richard Felstead.
June, 1980.

LIST OF ILLUSTRATIONS

Jack's grandmother collecting Parish relief from the workhouse.

Jack (left), with cousin Rhys, outside Aunt Elizabeth's home in Abertridwr, 1913.

Chapter 1

Mabon's Child

" Hail bounteous May, that doth inspire
Mirth, and youth, and warm desire."
John Milton.

May's gentle breezes breathe life into the yawning world of
nature, blowing away winter's sleepdust. The first garden crops
stretch their shoots through the softening soil. Trees, fields, hedge-
rows and plants don their new party dresses.

The first day of May has been celebrated from ancient times,
and in medieval England maypoles were erected in parks and on
village greens. Young men collected flowers from the woods and
made garlands to trim the poles. Maidens, as fertile as Spring,
sported their new gowns hoping to be chosen as the May queen.
The honoured girl danced around the maypole, her subjects holding the ribbon-ends that waxed from its peak in a sea of colour.

In 1889, the socialist parties of the world chose May the first as
the day when working people everywhere could show their solidarity
by holding mass parades.

By some remarkable coincidence, a decade later, on the first day
of May, 1899, when nature was rubbing its sleepy eyes, John
Roberts was born in the Merionethshire village of Penrhyndeudraeth.

Jack spent his boyhood in this lovely village on the border of
Merioneth and Caernarfon. It was a boy's paradise. Snowdonia's
stark mountains stood guard like sentinels in the distance. The
Dwyryd, Teigl and Glaslyn rivers flowed into the sea, forming an
estuary a stone's throw away from the village. The young Jack
played on the twin beaches of Traeth Mawr and Traeth Bach,

1

The Senghennydd Disaster, October 1913. A wife waits for news.

swam, climbed, birdnested, and met the village menfolk when they returned home from their toil at the Blaenau Ffestiniog slate quarries.

A long, steep hill separated Upper and Lower Penrhyndeudraeth. During the summer months, scores of tourists passed through the village on their bicycle rambles of North Wales. Jack would wait at the bottom of the hill, ready to accost the perspiring excursionists with the only English phrase he knew :

" Push your bike, sir ? "

It wasn't often that his labours went unrewarded.

Jack had reason to curse the hill, too. His grandfather had been a blacksmith in Harlech before his health broke. After retiring to Penrhyndeudraeth he used his smithy skills to make himself a tricycle. It was an odd contraption. He pedalled the cycle with his hands, while resting his feet on the running boards which flanked the weird conveyance. If his grandfather could make a bike, so could he, concluded Jack. Out of an abandoned perambulator he made a boneshaker. A dangerous, wobbly structure that defied all laws of locomotion. And where better to test-run the bike than on the hill ? A friend held the bike steady at the top of the hill. Jack mounted and a hefty push sent him on his way. The bike went out of control and Jack gritted his teeth as Lower Penrhyndeudraeth neared at an uncomfortable rate. At the bottom of the hill was a General Stores. Luckily, the door was open and Jack shot through the porch hurling biscuit tins in all directions. Unluckily, the shop owner was the local Justice of the Peace.

Jack didn't like school and he truanted whenever he could. Discipline was too strict for the fun-loving boy. Penrhyndeudraeth County School did not appreciate Jack's pranks. He released a frog in class to frighten the girls and received a severe beating from the headmaster. Jack's grandmother, Sarah Jones, secured his transfer to the village Church School. Although well intentioned, it proved a calamitous move. The headmistress was young and small in stature and the older boys terrorized her. Jack mitched for weeks on end.

One day, when he was twelve, Jack met Twm Dinas Mawddwy on the way to school. Twm showed a half ounce of tobacco he'd acquired. No school that morning. Down to the beach they went with their tobacco and the currants Jack had stolen from his grandmother's kitchen. Jack returned home lunchtime to find Sarah frying onions. She had intended baking a cake, but the currant jar was empty. Did Jack know anything about it ? Jack felt very ill. Waves of nausea flowed over him. Currants, tobacco juice and the smell of frying onions proved too much. There was no point in trying to deny the theft because Jack vomited the evidence on to the kitchen floor. On the mantelpiece Sarah kept a single birch. She took it down. Jack took down his trousers.

Jack loved his grandmother dearly and enjoyed sitting on her knee listening to how she had helped her blacksmith husband strike new horseshoes in the flaming brazier, sharpen scythe blades and tyre cartwheels .The heart of Jack's later political philosophy sprang from his hatred of officialdom he first encountered in the treatment of his grandmother. When her husband died, Sarah was forced to apply to the local parish for relief. After a strict means test she was allowed 2s. 9d. a week on which to eke out a miserable existence. To add to her humiliation, she was expected to walk one and a half miles along the Maentwrog road to collect her pittance at the prisonlike workhouse. Jack abhorred the system which demanded that his frail old grandmother completed the weekly three mile round trek in all weathers. The God-fearing mother of ten children trudging her arthritic legs to the workhouse, the cold, grey monument to a nation's warped conscience, an ever-present reminder of the miseries of pauperism.

In 1908, Lloyd George, the Chancellor of the Exchequer, carried through Parliament a Bill which introduced Old Age Pensions of five shillings per week for the over seventies who were both needy and worthy. Sarah Jones walked like a queen to the village Post Office to collect her entitlement. A proud woman again. The stigma of the Parish and bitter humiliation of the workhouse removed.

In 1913, Jack was old enough to leave school and his grandmother arranged for him to move to the village of Abertridwr, in South Wales. Her daughter, Elizabeth, had moved there from Blaenau Ffestiniog some years previously. Jack would be happy there with his aunt, Sarah said. His uncle would find him a job in the pit. There was a future in coal.

Sarah Jones had realised the significance of her failing health. Jack moved to Abertridwr in August 1913. He returned briefly to his native Penrhyndeudraeth a few days after Christmas, to put flowers on the grave of the woman who had reared him.

4

August 1913. Bombardier Wells, the heavyweight champion of Great Britain, knocked out Pat O'Keefe in the fifteenth round, with seven rounds to spare. Mrs. Pankhurst was released from Holloway Prison. Suffragettes fought with police in Trafalgar Square. The King went grouse shooting at Studley Royal, and Seccombes of Cardiff offered their summer millinery at clearing prices.

The sun shone nearly every day polishing the roofs of the little terraced houses that clung to the mountainside in the Aber valley. Abertridwr worked, played, worshipped and loved, each with an equal ardour and Jack, fourteen years of age, five foot nothing and seven stone, moved into the home of his aunt Elizabeth.

Jack started work in the recently sunk Windsor Colliery, Abertridwr. There was a future in coal, his grandmother had said, but after only two months in South Wales, Jack the young collier boy, learned the true price of coal. It was measured in blood, not hundredweights and tons.

Tuesday, October 14th, started like any other day in the valley. Men and youths on the morning shift at the twin pits of the Windsor and the Universal Colliery, Senghennydd, were at work. Mothers prepared breakfast for their children before they went to school. At ten minutes past eight an explosion ripped through the valley.

Jack had been down the Windsor since six o'clock and had started a long day of shovelling coal into drams. An urgent-voiced colliery official appeared. Everyone to the surface. Quickly. Explanations later. Jack looked forward to the prospect of the autumn sunshine. Happy to escape the dust-laden darkness. Rumours were rife at the pithead and upon returning home he learned of the catastrophe. Aunt Elizabeth was worried. Her brother Dai worked at the Universal. Had he been underground when the pit exploded ?

Jack walked to Senghennydd. Anxious crowds had gathered around the pit entrance for the second time in twelve years. In 1901, eighty-one men lost their lives in an explosion. Only one was saved.

The Universal was a new pit with a bad record. One of the most dangerous collieries in the coalfield. She was a bitch, capricious and gassy.

Jack arrived at his uncle's home, relieved to find him there preparing to take part in the rescue operations. Jack returned home to put his aunt's mind at peace.

5

The police had cordoned off the area around the pit and blocked the access roads. Women thronged around, awaiting news of husbands, sons, fathers, brothers. Rescue teams rushed to and fro. Bodies were being carted to makeshift mortuaries. Clergymen were comforting those to whom the certainty of bereavement had come. Jack pushed his way through the crowd. Black-faced, in working clothes, and coming from the direction of the pit, the women thought he was a survivor. A survivor. There was still hope. They cheered him and patted him on the head and shoulders.

As the day wore on, even the most optimistic abandoned hope. The manhood of the village and beyond was lost in a cavern of dreadful disaster. It was an exception to discover a home which had not been shrouded by tragedy. Four hundred and thirty nine men and boys died and that night two hundred wives went to bed without the comforting warmth of a husband. Twice as many children pined for their fathers. Senghennydd was a village of drawn blinds:

" O God, be Thou, on life's rough way
Our guide, our guardian, and our stay ;
On land, on sea, and 'neath the ground,
Where at their post true hearts are found.
Hear us, O Lord, Thine ear incline,
For those in peril in the mine."

Idris (Western Mail).

Outside the pit, Jack's life revolved around three centres. The Workmen's Hall with its billiard room, skittle alley, reading room and domino tables was popular with the miners.

Popular, too, was Bracchi the Italian's shop with its large, high stove in the centre of the shop-floor. Winter would drive in the crowds to enjoy a smoke, cup of hot Bovril and a cosy chat. Summer sent in the same crowds for the best home-made ice-cream in the area.

Inevitably, the third centre was the chapel, and Jack's interest in religion suddenly revived in 1916. He became interested in a girl who sat in the family pew opposite his. Her name was May Jones.

May's father was an ex-Porthmadog sailor who had sailed with the brig and schooner fleet carrying slate around the European coastal line. Mam Jones, May's mother, bewitched by the magic sound of foreign places, knew more about the port towns of the world than she did of Caerphilly or Pontypridd. Slate exports

6

slumped early in the century and Mam and Dad Jones moved from their home in Penrhyndeudraeth to Abertridwr.

Jack began his courtship on Sunday nights after the evening sermon. May possessed three important qualifications. She was from Penrhyndeudraeth, spoke Welsh and was pretty.

Three years later, on the morning of April 3, 1920 Jack walked the mile journey from Abertridwr to Eglwysilan Church. May followed on, whilst Mam Jones prepared a wedding breakfast for the young couple and few guests.

Jack and May, newly-wed proud, came out of the church and kissed in the porch. A few yards to their left was the grave of the Reverend William Edwards, minister and master bridge-builder. William Edwards made three attempts before succeeding in building a bridge over the River Taff at Pontypridd. Each time the hungry river carried it away. The newlyweds knew nothing of the great torrent of water that would, during the next decade, batter the bridge which spanned their lives :

> " April, April,
> Laugh thy girlish laughter ;
> Then, the moment after,
> Weep thy girlish tears."
> *Sir William Watson.*

After a fortnight's honeymoon in North Wales, May and Jack returned to Abertridwr to share Mam and Dad Jones' terraced house.

During the Great War, the government took control of the mines as a war measure. In 1919, after the German defeat, a Royal Commission was appointed to investigate the coal-mining industry. The Commission recommended continued government control of the mines, a reduction of working hours and an increase in colliers' wages.

Thunder clouds darkened the land as the coalowners and government combined to sweep the Sankey Commission recommendations under their grubby carpet.

The owners posted up notices of new conditions of employment when the government relinquished control on March 31, 1921. The next day a million miners throughout the country were locked-out. Deceived. April-fooled.

7

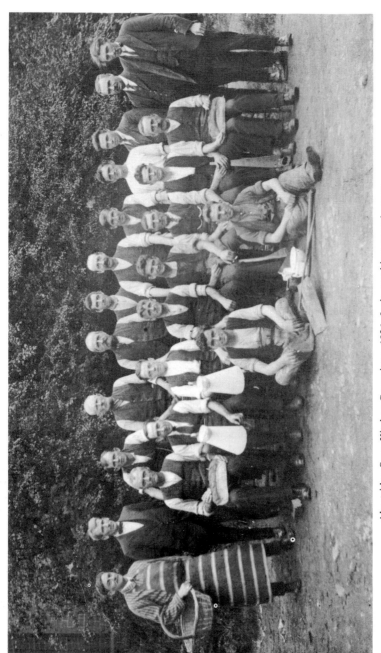

Abertridwr Soup Kitchen Committee, 1926. Jack, smoking, seated centre.

Dad Jones and Jack stayed at home with the women. Through the front bay window they gazed at the gaunt, motionless machinery of the Windsor pithead. They watched men wandering the streets, children carrying sticks to the soupkitchen, troops marching through the coalfield, police escorting blacklegs to work. And May grew larger with the child she was carrying. They saw the birth of a daughter. They saw her die two days later. They watched for three workless months, until the miners returned to work for reduced wages.

In 1921, Alfred Onions, the Member of Parliament for the Caerphilly constituency, died. The Labour Party nominated Mr. Morgan Jones, a Bargoed schoolmaster, to contest the seat. The newly-formed Communist Party decided to participate in the election. Its nomination was given to Bob Stewart, one of the party's founder members. Mr. Stewart had come to South Wales to speak to the miners during the recent stoppage. He was arrested and sentenced to three months' imprisonment at Cardiff Gaol. Released early in August he took Caerphilly by storm, speaking in the chief centres of the scattered constituency. Bob Stewart and a feast of Communist Party speakers addressed meetings.

Jack listened.

Theirs was the party that stood solidly by the workers. They had represented the miners during the strike. Their members were sentenced to terms of imprisonment for telling the truth, in the interests of the colliers. Theirs was the party that was unwilling to compromise. And what about the Labour Party ? What about the seventy Labour members in the House of Commons ? They took their salaries, but were unwilling to take the risks.

Powerful. Convincing. Effective. With the memory of the strike still a gangrenous wound in his mind, Jack began to think.

On 24 August 1921, the constituents went to the polling booths. Jack was amongst the thousands who assembled to await the result outside the Council Offices. At 3.20 the following morning the returning officer declared Morgan Jones the winner. But the two and a half thousand votes polled by Bob Stewart showed that the miners in the constituency were looking for an alternative party. Jack certainly was. He joined the Communist Party :

" And many a gilded tower
And many a palace steep,
Shall crumble in that hour
When Labour wakes from sleep."

9

The next five years were ones of struggle and in 1926, the storm broke over the land. The coal-owners proposed new agreements which threatened miners with the prospect of reduced wages and a longer working day.

From midnight on May 3rd, the miners, supported by the Trades Union Congress, brought the country to a nine-day standstill.

The Windsor Colliery became an industrial mute. Not a single wheel turned. Abertridwr railway station locked its gates. The Council bus service hibernated in its garages. Local industry and transport was crippled. The story was the same throughout the country.

After nine days, the T.U.C. called off the General Strike. The nation's miners were isolated. Betrayed and bitter, they settled down for a long struggle :

> " What will you do with your shovel, Dai
> And your pick and your sledge and your spike,
> And what will you do with your leisure, man,
> Now that you're out on strike ? "
>
> *Idris Davies.*

Local organisations throughout the coalfields organised sports and entertainments to preserve morale. Jack, a native Welsh speaker, was in demand to adjudicate recitations at the eisteddfodau. Young girls dressed in makeshift Welsh costumes and forgot their lines. Babies contended for the dubious distinction of being the bounciest. Whole families marched in carnival. Red Indians. Cowboys. Arabs wrapped up in front-room curtains. Fathers played rugby, football or puffed a hundred-yard dash before racing to the Workmen's Hall to watch Senghennydd's Tommy Jones outpointing Abertridwr's Billy Meade in the weekly boxing bout.

And there were the Jazz Bands. The mottled crews of colliers blazing their bazooka defiance. The Aber ' Coons ' trained on the exposed mountain slopes of Eglwysilan. Twice a week they marched and played, and Jack joined their ranks. After a few competition successes, the former Great War sergeant, who trained the ' Coons ' in marching and deportment, became more selective. Jack was one of the first to fall by the regimental wayside. But often, lying in bed late on a Saturday night, he and May would hear the triumphant band marching through the village. Sometimes it woke their four year old daughter, Margaret, from her dreams :

10

> " Brass bands in all the valleys
> Blaring defiant tunes,
> Crowds, acclaiming carnival
> Prize pigs and wooden spoons."
> *Idris Davies.*

Morale oozed through the pores of the valley. The weather was glorious. God, remarked the miners, was on their side. Charitable organisations donated money. The Russians sent financial aid to the Miners' Federation. The Canteen Fund was swollen with money from organised entertainments :

> " Only a penny, boys bach,
> And a concert first class,
> So roll up now with your pennies
> And help towards tomorrow's soup."
> *Idris Davies.*

Jack shared his time amongst the various activities connected with the Soup Kitchen preparations. In the early morning darkness he stole small coal, pit-props and railway sleepers from off the Windsor Colliery premises. Then there was a fire to build ; vegetables to be collected from gardens and allotments ; meat from the butcher. Cauldrons of stew tasted like the ambrosia of the gods. Morale crackled like the pit-prop fire. The coal owners would be beaten yet :

> " The summer wanes and the wine of words
> Departs with the departing birds."
> *Idris Davies.*

Summer over, the trees began to weep their leaves. Tommy Jones was still beating Billy Meade in their weekly encounter. Batches of children left the valley to live with London families for the remainder of the strike. Tommy followed them to box London's lightweights. The local miners' choir toured the South of England. They sang their hearts out to fill their children's bellies :

> " And here we came tramping and singing
> Out of the valleys of strife,
> Into the sunlit cornlands,
> Begging the bread of life."
> *Idris Davies.*

Winter drained Autumn's dregs. Bad weather came. Rain and floods spoiled the sports meetings and carnivals. Bootless children were unable to go to school. The canteen fund dried up. Prospects were as bleak as winter.

In November, six months of poverty and hardship forced the miners back to their pits. They accepted longer hours and lower wages. The government and coal owners were the victors.

'Jack Russia' addressing miners at the Windsor Colliery.

Chapter 2

Jack Russia

" I am a little man and this is a little town
but there must be a spark in a little man
that can burst into flame."

John Steinbeck (The Moon is Down).

May was ill, very ill. She had been unwell for the six years since
the General Strike. She felt spiritless and washed-out. Her skin
assumed a deathly white pallor. She heard noises in her ears, was
short of breath and frequently felt faint. The doctor was a regular
visitor to the house as May's strength ebbed. He diagnosed
pernicious anaemia, the most difficult of all anaemias to treat.

American doctors were experimenting with a new therapy and
May, in a desperate attempt to produce the healthy red-blood cells
she needed so badly, consumed mountains of raw and semi-cooked
beef liver. But the new treatment had come too late. May's condition was so advanced that the diagnosis of pernicious anaemia was
the equivalent of a death sentence.

A fortnight before Christmas 1932, May's health deteriorated
further and she was unable to get out of bed. It was a bad Christmas. Bad for Jack, bad for ten year old Margaret and bad for Mam
Jones. May would not see another.

On Friday evening, December 31, the last day of 1932, as the
village prepared to toast the New Year and as throats were cleared
to sing *Auld Lang Syne,* May, shroud-white, an old woman at 34,
found a final peace :

"Sleep away the years,
Sleep away the pain,
Wake, tomorrow,
A girl again."

Hal Summers.

The week after, May was buried at Penyrheol Cemetery, Caerphilly. The rest of the family went about the difficult business of living.

One evening, after returning from a walk, Jack found Mam Jones and Margaret huddled in front of a fireless grate. January was a cold month. Colder still, because of their loss.

Jack went out again. Across the road from the house to the Windsor Colliery coalbank. In the darkness he filled a sack with small coal and sawed two wooden railway sleepers into portable blocks. They could now, at least, mourn in warmth.

The following afternoon, William Hughes, a friend of the family, came to pay his respects and before leaving, Jack gave him a sack of firewood. As Bill was crossing the village square on his way home, he was stopped by Police Constable Grace. He demanded to know what was in the sack. Bill replied truthfully but refused to say where he had acquired it.

Later that afternoon, P.C. Grace, accompanied by the steamroller bulk of Sergeant Williams, knocked on the door of Bill's Brook Street house. It was opened by Bill's wife and young son:

"Where has your husband been this afternoon, Mrs. Hughes?" asked the Sergeant.

Before she had time to reply, her son, eager to help, answered:

"Dad went up to see Jack Roberts, to take back the bowler hat he borrowed to go to the funeral."

There was a knock on the door of 28 Church Road, sometime afterwards. When Jack answered, P.C. Grace and Sergeant Williams filled the porch:

"We want to know about some firewood. Have you got any?"

Jack's negative reply failed to convince them. They forced their way through the house and climbed the steps which led to the coalshed in the back garden. Two other policemen entered the garden from the lane behind the house. Sergeant Williams rummaged in the shed and found a pile of small coal and sawn-up sleeper blocks.

The police escorted Jack to Senghennydd Police Station. Bill Hughes was already there.

16

Police escorting blackleg through Trethomas, March 1933.

During the first week of February, at Caerphilly Police Court, Jack was found guilty of stealing small coal valued at 3s. 2d. and two wooden sleepers worth four shillings. He was fined ten shillings on each charge. Bill was fined ten shillings for receiving stolen timber.

Jack's hatred of the ruling classes deepened. They had killed his wife. They were responsible, theirs was the guilt.

They had also taken his job away. Victimised him. There was a virtue in being regarded a good and regular workman. The coal-seams lay under the ground he trod. He wanted to work, but the owners wouldn't let him. There was a personal pride in providing for one's family, but May was dead.

No wife. No job. It was a double pronged attack upon his manhood. Jack felt as worthless as the clinker tips that scarred the village.

He was not alone in his frustration. The Depression was making the village a cemetery. Breadwinners were out of work. They lounged around the street corners watching the long hours drain away. It was hard on the women, feeding their families from empty larders. Clothes were threadbare and patched. Their houses were in need of repair and a fresh coat of paint. No coal to heat their homes, yet millions of tons under their feet.

Hundreds of families were moving away from the dereliction of the valleys to areas of greater economic stability.

Thousands remained and accepted their lot.

A handful became rebels. Neighbouring villages had their Emlyn 'Kremlin' and 'Bolshy' Watkins. Abertridwr had its Jack ' Russia,' crying out, soap-box high, against the injustices he saw around him. The lieutenants of those who caused his oppression lay within his grasp : the colliery owners and their officials, the police and the magistrates. Jack began to challenge their authority with all the force his body and mind could muster.

Inevitably, Jack was in constant trouble with the police. Sergeant Williams was a regular caller to the house. Jack's court appearances were numerous and he boasted to have paid enough money in fines to shoe the whole of the Glamorgan Constabulary. Finding the money was always a problem but enterprising friends and family usually came to the rescue. On one occasion, Jack's sister-in-law, Nell, raffled two geese she'd been fattening for Christmas : " Christmas is coming, the goose is getting fat, please put a penny in the old man's hat. . . . ."

Saturday, March 18, 1933.

Wearing a pair of fashionable Harris Tweed plus-fours and an open necked khaki shirt, Jack set out on a borrowed bicycle to sell Communist Party raffle tickets in Nantgarw. Arriving at the foot of the steep Cwrtrawlin Hill outside Caerphilly, he dismounted and began to push. It was cold and a strong headwind blew into his face. Impulsively, Jack decided against continuing to Nantgarw and opted for the easier, slightly down hill ride to Bedwas. He could see how the villagers were receiving the blacklegs as they came off the morning shift.

Bedwas had been a trouble spot for some years and in February 1933, the colliers went on strike. It was a protest against the colliery company's policy of employing newcomers at the expense of long term employees. Within a month of the strike, over five hundred outsiders were signed on and made to join a blackleg union in an attempt to break the strike.

Blacklegging was one of the greatest social and industrial problems of the decade. Villages were divided into warring factions and an uneasy war developed between the unemployed and the ' scabs.' Their windows were smashed or tarred. Wreaths were placed at their doorsteps. They were waylaid on their way to work, ducked in streams. Coping stones were prised off railway bridges on to trains conveying them to work. They lived in constant fear and were escorted by the police to and from their work.

In communities where mass unemployment was the order of the day, the blackleg was public enemy number one, a cancer—evil, malignant and crippling. He stole another man's job, was a traitor to his own kind, a tool of the company, an expendable pawn in an acrimonious game of industrial chess.

Jack arrived at Trethomas at half past two and stood in anticipation with the gathering crowd of unemployed and their wives.

Four blacklegs and a police escort of six left the premises of the Bedwas Navigation Colliery. They passed the school. Today it was quiet. During the week, the children climbed the school railings in their playtime to yell abuse at the passing blacklegs. Quiet today, it was Saturday.

At three o'clock, the blacklegs reached the main road and the policemen on strike duty escorted John Davies to his home in Coronation Street. A huge crowd lined the street to humiliate him as he passed. They booed and hissed and the women laughed their scorn :

> " They take their picks and down they go,
> To dig out coal tha's lying below,
> And there isn't a woman in this town row
> Will look at a blackleg miner."
>
> *Traditional Ballad.*

The crowd followed John Davies home, shouting " Rotter ! " " Scamp ! " " Traitor ! "

Mrs. Emily Parry, the wife of a Federation man who'd been laid off, tried to break through the police cordon. A constable tripped her up. Mrs. Mary Ludlow went to help her friend and neighbour but was roughly pushed aside by another policeman. In retaliation she began kicking and shouting at the police. The mood of the crowd was becoming increasingly ugly and hostile.

Superintendent Spendlove ordered the arrest of the women.

" Don't lock them up," yelled an incensed crowd.

A band of policemen closed around the women in a protective circle and began conveying them the half mile to Bedwas Police Station.

Outside Trethomas Workmen's Hall was an empty council bus and its driver. Mesdames Ludlow and Parry were violently pushed on board. Mrs. Ludlow struck her head on the floor.

The bus driver was so terrified he scrambled from his cab taking the ignition keys with him.

Willam Milsom, the secretary of the Bedwas lodge, was working inside the Workmen's Hall when he heard the commotion outside. Approaching the bus to investigate, he saw a sergeant and another policeman holding Mary Ludlow down in between two seats.

" Please let the woman get up. I'll be responsible for the crowd and will accompany her to the police station," pleaded Milsom.

" I'm sorry," replied the sergeant, " but I have got my orders, I cannot let her go."

The crowd now numbered over eight hundred. Armed with stones and sticks they ran, frenzied and shouting, along an adjacent banking and piece of waste ground.

Jack was caught in the torrential flow of the crowd. He neared the bus and saw Mary Ludlow and Emily Parry, distressed and dishevelled. Catching hold of Superintendent Spendlove's arm, Jack advised :

Jack with daughter Margaret upon his release from Cardiff Gaol, November, 1933

"You let these women go, Super. Look at the frenzy of the crowd. They will kill you before you get there."

Spendlove brushed Jack aside and ordered that the women be taken on foot to the Police Station.

The women, their police escort and swelling crowd of a thousand reached Bedwas Square. Someone threw a stone at a policeman. Spendlove retaliated. He ordered his constables to charge the crowd with their batons. The police hit out in all directions, and in the ensuing mêlée half a dozen policemen and twenty others were injured.

Jack was standing in the middle of the road near the Police Station. A truncheoned policeman walked with a slow deliberate step towards him. Instinctively looking to his rear Jack saw another policeman closing in. He tried to dive around the back of the constable but was caught across the shoulders by a glancing blow. Jack stumbled into the gutter but quickly regained his balance and made good his escape.

The show was over. The villain of the melodrama locked himself in the safety of his Coronation Street home. The two leading ladies were being charged inside Bedwas Police Station and the thousand extras left the scene. The police returned their blue costumes to their wardrobes. A variety of props scattered the stage—an abandoned bus outside the Workmen's Hall and a carpet of stones and sticks covered Bedwas Square. It was a Gala Performance which received rave reviews in the local press.

The following Tuesday, Jack was waiting with a crowd of sixty others outside the chemist shop in Thomas Street, Abertridwr. They were waiting for the bus which transported village blacklegs from their work at Bedwas Colliery. The bus arrived and twenty blacklegs alighted. The first to come parallel with the jeering crowd was Trevor James. He appeared to be lame, white bandages showing through his ripped trousers.

Still burning with a white-hot indignation at the events of the previous Saturday, Jack crossed the road, shouting :

"They are a lot of wasters. Here is one of the blacklegs. Let's give him a cheer, boys."

Trevor James was frightened by the hostility of the crowd. Still recovering from the shock of a slight underground accident that day, he was at collapsing point when Jack reached him outside Beulah Chapel. Realising that something was wrong, Jack held

Windsor Colliery, Abertridwr, 1930.

James up against the chapel railings to prevent him falling to the pavement. It was unfortunate for Jack that the ever-present Sergeant Williams witnessed the scene.

Events began to move rapidly for Jack. The sands of his time were running out.

Later that week he was served with a summons to appear in Bedwas Court to answer charges relating to the Bedwas Riots.

On April 4th, Jack was charged in Caerphilly Police Court with intimidation with violence and besetting Trevor James in Abertridwr. He was fined £10 (or 41 days imprisonment) on each of the two charges and allowed four months to pay the fines.

A week to the day later, Jack appeared in Bedwas Police Court. More than seventy people were summoned there to hear evidence connected with the Bedwas dispute. Jack was one of the twenty four committed for trial at Monmouthshire Assizes in June. He was allowed bail on his own recognizance of £10.

Shortly after Whitsun, the twenty four appeared at Monmouthshire Assizes. For four days they stood in the enlarged dock wearing a number around their necks. They were jointly accused with riotously assembling at Trethomas and Bedwas on March 18th " and then did make great riot and disturbance to the terror and alarm of His Majesty's subjects."

The jury deliberated for an hour and a quarter, and it was nearly eight o'clock on a Friday evening when Mr. Justice Lawrence passed sentence. Of the twenty four accused, four women and seven men were sentenced to terms of imprisonment varying from one to six months. Jack received a six month sentence.

After the names of those found guilty were announced Police Superintendent Spendlove proclaimed that " Roberts who was a native of North Wales was described in that area as a most vicious and violent man."

A most vicious and violent man ! Quite a record for a lad who left Penrhyndeudraeth at the age of thirteen. Jack's greatest crime was truanting. The long arm of the law stretching back three decades.

As the prisoners were escorted to the cells, Lil Price, who together with her husband Goff, was sentenced to four months' imprisonment, shouted :

" Down with fascism ! Three cheers for the Bedwas Strike. We cannot get justice."

On the afternoon of the riot Lil had popped out of the house to find her young son. She had taken no active part in the disorder. She was pinpointed because she was a Communist Party member. Workers in Bedwas were furious at the sentences. Furious, too, at Spendlove's slanderous attack upon Jack. Jack was described as the most violent agitator under the Superintendent's jurisdiction, and an agent provocateur, a Moscow boy pouring petrol on the political bonfire.

The Central Committee of the Communist Party pledged to rally its whole membership to enforce the release of the Bedwas prisoners. It was a shout in the wilderness. The population of H.M. Prison, Cardiff, was temporarily increased by eleven.

One of the fables attributed to the Greek slave Aesop tells of how a father demonstrated the importance of unity to his bickering sons. Individual tree-twigs could be snapped with ease. Collectively they could not. Unity, proved the father, was strength.

The South Wales Miners' Federation had been weakened during the decade following the General Strike, as ' scab ' unionism gained a foothold in the valleys. The only salvation of the workers was through Trade Union unity. Federation unity was the workers' strength.

Periodical checks on Federation membership were made. Lodge officials would conduct a ' show cards,' a check of colliers' contribution cards. Such a measure, unpopular with the coal owners, would reveal non-Federation members and those in arrears with their payments.

In September 1934, a year after his release from Cardiff Prison, Jack, with other lodge officials, held a ' show cards ' at the Windsor Colliery. Committee men stood at all the colliery approach roads and outside the lamproom hatches.

Suddenly, Badger, the pit-manager, appeared in a rage. He toppled the tables which were being used for collecting contributions and ordered the union officials off the colliery premises. The men left, but not before one, Dick Hughes, miner, lay-preacher and sworn enemy of profanities had his say. Clasping his hands in prayer, and looking heavenwards, he invoked :

" Holy Father, close thine sacred ears for five minutes while I tell this ignorant bugger what I think of him, in his own language."

What followed is unprintable.

25

The Powell Duffryn Steam Coal Company complained that the ' showcards ' and pithead meetings were a trespass. The law of the land agreed and a High Court injunction to restrain trespass on the Windsor Colliery premises was granted by Mr. Justice Clauson on November 6th, 1935.

Soon afterwards, Jack crossed the pit, taking his customary shortcut to Senghennydd Labour Exchange. He had broken the terms of the injunction and was, subsequently, handed a summons by the colliery sergeant. He was to appear at the Central Criminal Court, popularly called the Old Bailey after the city street in which it stands.

Jack entered through the Court's wrought iron gates into the muraled and statued Edwardian palace, which occupies the blood-stained site of what was once Newgate Prison.

Seeing a court official engrossed in some paperwork near a huge staircase, Jack approached and showed his summons. The official read it and explained its details to someone on the telephone.

" This summons is inaccurate," he said. " Your case will be dismissed on a technicality. You can't be brought here again on this summons and because you are unemployed you should have received expenses to come."

Jack could not believe his good fortune.

Upon returning to Abertridwr, Daniel Walter Thomas, the local mines examiner, called to the house :

" I see you got away with it, then, Jack. I was just talking to Badger, the Manager. He was fuming. Hopping bloody mad ! Said it cost the company a hundred quid."

Jack was pleased to think that he was a thorn in the Powell-Duffryn flesh and re-crossed the colliery premises on his next weekly visit to the Senghennydd Labour Exchange.

Jack's deliberate provocation earned him a second summons and a further trip to London, shortly before Christmas. Leaving home at four-o'clock on a freezing December morning, he walked the ten miles to Cardiff in order to catch the early morning London train. The Fishguard–Paddington express was delayed and Jack arrived in court late. Dishevelled and out of breath after his dash across London, he explained :

" Sorry, I'm late. I didn't mean to be in contempt of court. I left home in plenty of time, but the mail-train was late because of a stormy Irish Sea crossing."

Mr. Justice Eve responded :

" Can you think of a better place to celebrate Christmas than in Brixton Prison ? "

" Yes, sir," replied Jack, " with my daughter and mother-in-law in the little village I walked from this morning."

Jack returned home a second time.

Sometime after Christmas, Jack was selling copies of the " Daily Worker " on the Windsor Colliery access road. Instead of remaining in one place he ambled up and down the path whilst waiting for the colliers to come off shift.

It was his third trespass. A third summons followed. London again, and Jack was frightened. The thought of Brixton clouded all his thoughts. Twice he'd beaten the coalowners. Three times was asking too much. The King's Counsel looked stern when he asked if Jack had ever been given the terms of the injunction.

" No," answered Jack.

" Well," continued the Justice, " you are not to set foot on the Windsor Colliery premises to conduct a ' showcards,' to attend pit-head meetings, to hold a ballot, to stick or exhibit posters, to distribute leaflets or to sell newspapers. You are not to go anywhere near the premises of the Windsor Colliery. I do not want to see you here again. Do you understand ? "

Jack couldn't believe his luck. He had expected the worst. But he was free. No Brixton for him. Almost skipping with joy he left the Court. Above the main door were inscribed the words :

" Defend the children of the poor and punish the wrongdoer."

Back home in Abertridwr, Jack became a folk-hero. To the miners and the unemployed he was the man who took on and beat the coalowners. To their children he was the reason for popularizing an old game. In Church Road, children trouped in lines underneath an arch made by two of the older children. They chanted :

> " Oranges and lemons
> Say the bells of St. Clement's.
>
> Your owe me five farthings,
> Say the bells of St. Martin's.
>
> When will you pay me ?
> Say the bells of Old Bailey."

In May 1935, the country celebrated the Silver Jubilee of King George V. Communities everywhere organised street parties. Children, sticky with jelly and blancmange, cheered, waved banners and lit bonfires. Caerphilly Castle was floodlit. So, too, were the Urban Distrcit Council Offices. The offices were, additionally, illuminated by Jack's election on to the Council. " I can visualize lively times in the Council Chamber," wrote one observer.

Jack first decided to stand as a Communist candidate in 1932. Mr. Dan Collins, the Labour Councillor, was seeking re-election and Jack's chances in a three-cornered fight were dismissed as being nil. The local press referred to his as " a freak candidature and not worthy of consideration." When Jack forced the Independent candidate into third place, the same newspaper commiserated with the Independent's mortification in seeing a Communist come second in the poll.

In 1933, in a stiff fight between Jack and the Labour candidate only eleven votes saved the Socialist Party from defeat.

Jack was unfortunate, in 1934, to stand against the bowler-hatted Independent Mr. William Rowland. He was a good public representative, had approved a scheme to provide swimming pools in each ward and was in favour of issuing season tickets on omnibuses. President of the Abertridwr branch of the British Legion and chairman of the Governors of Caerphilly Miners' Hospital, his return was a foregone conclusion.

In 1935, Dan Collins resigned and the Labour banner was carried by Daniel Walter Thomas. Jack, inevitably, carried the Red Flag. It was a straight contest between the two. Jack's election campaign was his most vigorous to date. He stood on walls and soapboxes throughout the village addressing street meetings. He spent hours canvassing and distributing election leaflets.

The night before polling day, whilst everyone in Abertridwr slept, he traipsed the village with a pocketful of coloured chalks, daubing his slogans on walls and doors. The more public places like major crossroads, polling booths and village square were plastered with huge slogans in white lime :

" Vote Jack Roberts, your Communist Candidate." " Jack ' Russia ' for Abertridwr."

The morning of the election dawned and the village was covered by a political rainbow. Jack wore a radiant smile of confidence and a mammoth red rosette. The people of Abertridwr went to the polling booths and Jack's arena moved off the streets and pithead into the Council Chamber. It was a great personal triumph and

Jack went on to represent the people of his ward on the Caerphilly Urban District Council for the next eighteen years.

It was quite a distinguished record for a freak who wasn't worthy of consideration as a political candidate.

In November 1936, Jack cheated. The third National Hunger March organised by the Unemployed Workers' Movement was converging on London. They came from all parts of the country to present a petition of a million signatures to the House of Commons. They demanded the abolition of the hated Means Test. Marchers spent many arduous weeks tramping the road to London. A contingent of five hundred represented South Wales. Jack cheated. He went by bike.

Jack was not included in the representation because of his council commitments. Unwilling to miss out on the event altogether he borrowed a bike and cycled to London with a friend, Ted Pitt.

They arrived at Hyde Park, the venue of the mass rally and traditional home of free speech, on Sunday morning November 8th. A crowd, numbering a quarter of a million, had assembled to listen to a host of speakers denounce the Means Test from half a dozen specially erected platforms. As Welsh Members of Parliament railed on their rostra against social injustice, marchers stood around chatting and smoking with family and friends who had moved to London to escape the dereliction of the valleys.

Many of the Welsh contingent went back to stay with sons, nephews and old workmates after the rally ended. The remainder, together with the two hunger-cyclists were provided with accommodation at Camberwell, south of the River Thames.

The next morning, Jack and Ted started their journey home. Mapless and uneducated in London geography, they were still lost within the metropolis maze at four in the afternoon.

Eventually, they followed the direction of a signpost marked Reading and cycled along the A4, as the November darkness enveloped the city.

The homeward journey was further hindered by Jack's bicycle lamp. It was a carbon lamp. Water dripped from a reservoir on to a bed of calcium carbide producing acetylene gas. The gas was ignited to produce the light-giving flame. That was the theory, but it was so bitingly cold that the water in Jack's tank froze.

Jack had, at some time, been told that urine freezes at a lower temperature than water. So, he urinated into the reservoir hoping

Hitler, Mussolini and Franco.

to melt the solid block of ice. It didn't work, so Jack had to continue his journey following the dim glow of Ted's bike.

They reached Gloucester during the early hours of the morning. The wind was howling like a hooligan. They were cold and exhausted, but cheered when they saw the welcome glimmer of an all-night transport café. Not wanting to run the risk of someone stealing their transport, Jack and Ted bundled in, wheeling their cycles.

The proprietor emerged from some seedy depth. His nose twitched accusingly. He saw Jack and demanded :

" Whose bike is that ? "

" Mine," replied Jack sheepishly.

" Well get the bloody thing out of here and stay out yourself, you filthy bugger."

Explanations proved futile. Nothing would convince the café owner that Jack didn't have trouble with his bladder.

Cold, hungry and insulted, Jack arrived home on Tuesday morning in time to sign the dole in Senghennydd Labour Exchange.

Chapter 3

The Last Great Cause

" So they came in long columns from all countries,
all who knew poverty well enough to die fighting it,
and some had guns and those who had no guns used
their hands, and one after another they came to lie
down on the earth of Spain."

André Malraux (Days of Hope)

Jack had reached a certain stage in his life. He had involved himself in the coalfield and unemployed battles. He was active in local politics, yet his plight remained unchanged. He was certainly no Samson vanquishing his oppressors with the jawbone of an ass.

Everywhere it was the same story. The weak oppressed by the strong.

In Italy, the father of fascism, Benito Mussolini, had declared the Socialists to be the betrayers of the nation. He contested that brute force was justified in eliminating political opposition, as blackshirted fascist squads roamed the country peddling their brand of violence.

In Austria, Chancellor Dollfuss was busy establishing a regime based on Italian fascist principles ; busy—castrating Austrian Socialism. The Socialists called a General Strike. Dollfuss executed its leaders and bombed the workers' flats in Vienna.

Next door in Hitler's Germany, the Third Reich abolished all political parties other than the National Socialists and the trade unions. Nazi strong arm bands goose-stepped out of some primeval horror. Guarantees of individual liberty were suspended as opponents were locked up behind the barbed wire of the concentration camps.

Wyndham 'Windy' Watkins with wife and son upon his return from Spain, 1938.

The Bullies were on the move throughout Europe. In October 1935, Mussolini's fascist juggernaut of motorised warfare invaded Ethiopia. Tanks and aircraft went on the warpath against feudal chiefs clad in lionskins. Cyclopes versus Lilliputians.

Then, in July 1936, the Spanish generals, backed by the armed might of Mussolini and Hitler, dealt a deadly blow to Iberian democracy. After an armed rebellion in Spanish Morocco, twenty thousand members of the Spanish Foreign Legion landed in Southern Spain. They marched on Madrid to overthrow the democratically elected government. General Franco confidently proclaimed " No earthly power can stop our triumphant movement. Spain is saved. Viva Espana."

The situation in Madrid was critical. Spain became the anti-fascist struggle.

Spain.

Spain was the syllable which began to engrave itself on Jack's mind. The clash in Spain was the logical extension of his battles at home. The fight of the Spanish people for democratic freedom was the fight of workers everywhere.

It was a struggle of light against darkness, liberty against dungeon chains.

Jack, at the cross-roads of his life, saw the signs clearly pointed. His road led to Spain. He joined the modern crusade of men from all over the world which converged on the Iberian Peninsula. He joined with the forty thousand who believed that Spain was the stage where democracy danced with death ; forty thousand who believed that Spain would be the cemetery of fascism.

Soon after returning from the Hunger March rally in London, Jack went to the Cardiff headquarters of the Communist Party and volunteered. He was turned down because he wasn't an ex-serviceman.

Jack returned in January 1937 with Wyndham " Windy " Watkins, an ex-serviceman and unemployed Abertridwr miner. It was agreed that they should go and they were given a London address as the first contact in the underground network, which existed to enable volunteers to reach Spain. Returning home, Jack spent a quiet evening with Mam Jones and Margaret. He gave no inclination of his intention. They couldn't begin to understand his motives.

At best, he would return home at the end of the war. At worst, the Spanish sun would bleach his bones. Next day, a gloomy January morning, Jack left Abertridwr without a word of farewell. His absence was his only adieu.

On arrival in London, Jack and Windy reported to the address they had been given. Half a dozen recruits were already in the house, and, after spending the night there, the group caught the boat-train to Paris. They travelled on a weekend-three day return ticket. They didn't need passports.

After spending two days in Paris, Jack boarded a train at the Gare d'Austerlitz for Perpignan, capital of the Pyrenees-Orientales department of south-east France. This former stronghold town and flourishing market centre was an ideal resting place for foreign recruits effecting an entry into Spain. It was only nineteen miles from the border.

They arrived in Perpignan, the pleasant tree-lined town where Spain overflows into France, on Sunday night. Jack and Windy followed their Paris contact from the station through the hunched evening streets to a tenement house in one of Perpignan's poorer quarters. There were six other volunteers in the house and they were all warned not to make themselves conspicuous around the town : stay in pairs ; no drunkenness ; no brothels ; strictly a low profile. One couldn't be overcautious now that the British government had made the Foreign Enlistment Act of 1870 applicable to the Spanish conflict. It was an offence for a British subject to accept, or agree to accept, any engagement in the military service of another country. Upon conviction, the penalty was a term of imprisonment of up to two years and a fine.

Keep a low profile.

Jack left the house in the company of Alun Menai Williams, the twenty-four year old son of the collier-poet Huw Menai.

Alun was born in Gilfach Goch, the village immortalised by Richard Llewellyn, in his novel ' How Green was my Valley.' The family later moved to Penygraig in the Rhondda Valley and it was from here that Alun, the unemployed miner, joined the Royal Army Medical Corps to escape the social devastation of the Rhondda. Unemployment. Army. Unemployed again. Alun went to live in London. An extract from his father's poem, ' Back in the Return ' describes what could have been Alun at this time :

> " Hungry, and penniless, an Out-of-Work,
> Who once the pose of dignity knew well,
> No longer now a stranger to the stoop
> That would the heartbreak tell."

36

Alun became a Labour Party activist in London. He sold copies of the ' Daily Worker ' on street corners. He took part in anti-fascist demonstrations. In January 1937, he went to the Communist Party National Headquarters at King Street and volunteered to fight for the Republican cause in Spain. Alun had no difficulty in being accepted. Here was an ex-serviceman with medical experience, and an imposing six foot three inch frame. Such credentials were rarely presented.

Jack and Alun wandered the streets of Perpignan, but were not at liberty for very long. They were approached by gendarmes, questioned, arrested and escorted to the ' Commissariat Central de Police.' Five of their comrades were already in custody. The only one of the group of eight who succeeded in evading the gendarmes was Jack's travelling companion from Abertridwr, ' Windy ' Watkins.

They were placed in a large, bare cell whose only concession to comfort was a straw pillow for each man. Being some of the first recruits to be arrested for contravening the provisions of the Foreign Enlistment Act they became prize-exhibits :—dinosaurs dragged up from some primeval forest. Officers of the French establishment fell over each other in their rush to photograph, fingerprint and make plaster casts of their prisoners' hands.

The Rhondda Valley town of Treherbert boasts a number of claims to fame. For instance there was the Treherbert Opera House, popular venue for operas, oratorios, concerts and eisteddfodau.

Once, the Operatic Society decided to produce Mendelssohn's famous oratorio ' Elijah,' which climaxed with Elijah ascending to heaven in a chariot of fire. Wishing to make the Hebrew prophet's heavenly ascent as realistic as possible the Society secured the aid of a colliery blacksmith. He rigged up a chariot manipulated by a series of pulleys and ropes. When the dramatic moment arrived, a rope snapped and Elijah crashed to the stage breaking a leg.

Elijah was not the only unfortunate to pile-drive the stage of the Treherbert Opera House. The place was also used for boxing contests and one of the greatest local crowd-pullers was Tommy Picton. A Treherbert miner, and ex-light heavyweight boxing champion of the Navy, he was twice decorated for bravery in the Great War. Tom guaranteed a packed Opera House. All would be there to watch him cruise the ring, deadly as a dreadnought, landlubbering his opponents to the deck.

Tom didn't belong to any political party. He wasn't active in working class demonstrations. But he did admire a fighter, and he saw the Communists as boxing-booth pugilists punching their way to a working class victory. Many Rhondda Communists were in Spain. There was a fight there and Tom had to be part of it.

Like Jack, Tom reached Perpignan only to be arrested under the terms of the Foreign Enlistment Act. He barely tolerated his imprisonment. He regarded the French police as unscrupulous promoters, trying to keep him out of the ring on the night of his big fight. As Tom snorted around the cell like an enraged steer the solution of his incarceration became increasingly clear.

" Look here, boys," Tom explained to his fellow captives, " there's no need for us to stay all cooped up in this sodding place. One of you tell the guard you want to go for a pee. When he comes to take you to the toilet I'll sling him a punch as he opens the cell-door. The bugger won't wake up for a fortnight. We'll take his gun and fight our way out of here."

Nobody doubted the sincerity of Tom's intentions. Although over fifty years of age, he was still built like a bull and his cauliflower ear bore testimony to one too many pugilistic encounters. Nobody, however, was either bold or rash enough to encourage Tom with his escape plot.

When he was later released, Tom reached Spain from where he sent home a letter to his friend George Thomas, Communist Councillor for Ton Pentre :

" I think George old boy that a bloody heap of the boys hanging around the corners should be here with me but anyway George I am bloody proud that I am here whatever the hell happens and we are bloody sure that we are going to win. We are not coming back until we drive these rats out of it. I was very popular at the Ystrad Police Station but I am very much more popular out here because of my mad stunts. They say, here comes the mad Taff. So I must go easy now or it will be like the old song—the ship that never returns. I have had some narrow goes here George believe me, but you can take it for granted, I have accounted for hell of a lot of fascists."

Tom foresaw his own end. The ship never returned, The pocket battleship was captured by the fascists and shot in a Franco Prison Camp. The Treherbert rough diamond died as he had lived—with a clenched fist.

Monday was spent in Perpignan prison. On Tuesday morning

five of the group were taken to a court in the town and defended by two women lawyers. Despite Tom Picton's colourful protestations that he was on holiday, too old to fight, deaf and going blind, the whole group was sentenced to fifteen days' imprisonment for vagabondage.

Jack and Alun were not charged with the others and on Wednesday evening they were released and put on a train for Marseilles, France's second largest city and chief Mediterranean port. They were escorted on their journey by a plain-clothes inspector of police who delivered them to the British Consulate-General at No. 1, rue d'Arcole.

After being shown into an ante-room, the sixty year old Consul-General, Lionel Edward Keyser appeared. The greying Cambridge University trained Keyser had moved to his present post some two years previously from the Consulate at Quito, the high Andean capital of Equador.

From the start of the encounter, Lionel Keyser adopted a disdainful and supercilious manner. He wanted nothing to do with them. They had contravened the British and French government's policy of non-intervention. They had broken the laws of two countries and were liable to a term of imprisonment not exceeding two years. They were criminals and he treated them as such. He questioned Jack and Alun in an endeavour to establish the route and contacts that had brought them to France.

Jack explained that they had come on a weekend trip to Paris to sample what dizzy delights France's premier city had to offer. They had got excessively drunk and lost their money. Somehow they ended up in Perpignan.

Keyser remained unconvinced. Alun and Jack didn't look the types who could afford to toast champagne in the Folies Bergères. The official representative of the British government in Marseilles refused even the slightest help in aiding their return home. Jack and Alun were hurriedly ushered out of the Consulate-General.

Soon after leaving the rue d'Arcole, a call of nature demanded that the Welshmen look for somewhere to obtain relief. They mistakenly climbed down a long flight of stone steps. Seated at the bottom was an old matron enraged to see two men in a ladies' sanctuary. She chased them back up the stairs and out into the street shrieking French threats that needed no translation.

Jack and Alun ran for their lives bumping into what seemed to be the whole of Marseilles' one million teeming population. Eventually they arrived at the sprawling hillside maze of Vieux Port, the slums dock area of the city that the Germans were to dynamite in 1943 because it was an active centre of the French Resistance.

The Welshmen passed through the street markets where the fishermen and their wives shouted the virtues of their catch, through the warren of narrow cobbled streets thronged with its cosmopolitan masquerade. They were hungry but passed a number of cafés on the waterfront Quai de Belges in favour of one which proudly proclaimed: " English Cooking Here." Jack had no desire to savour the local ' bouillabaise,' a garlic and saffron flavoured fish stew. He felt safer with an English dish. The café was a jumble of tables and chairs and smelt strongly of black coffee and cognac. Feeling safe in the noisy privacy of the café, Jack launched a most uncomplimentary tirade against Lionel Edward Keyser and the government he represented. He and Alun had no money, no knowledge of French and had been refused aid by their only contact with home. If Jack had only known! On a snow-white limestone island outside Marseilles harbour was the celebrated prison of the Man in the Iron Mask and the Count of Monte Cristo. There Jack would have certainly wished the British Consul to languish for the remainder of his natural life in one of the dampest underground cells of the infamous Chateau d'If.

In the middle of this outburst, Jack was approached by an Englishwoman who had overheard his verbal tantrum. She was able to give the address of a British Seaman's chaplain who operated a Mission in the Vieux Port. Retracing their steps through the hillside honeycomb of slums, Jack and Alun found the cassocked chaplain. He listened sympathetically to their predicament, allowed them refuge in the Mission and agreed to cable a telegram to Jack's friend, Trevor Owen. Trevor was the Clerk of the Caerphilly District Council, and Jack cabled requesting money to cover his passage home to Wales.

Some days later, an announcement came over the Mission tannoy system. Would Messrs. Roberts and Williams report to the Chaplain. Trevor Owen had sent the necessary funds and Jack and Alun were able to catch the evening train for Paris.

They had to change trains at the railway centre of Toulouse. With time in hand whilst awaiting their connection, the Welshmen went to have a snack in the station café. From where he sat Jack saw a fellow alight from an incoming train. No-one could have been in any doubt of his intention. Wearing a serge suit adorned with ribboned medals he was shouting ' Viva Espana Valiente. Viva la Republica ' with a lack of caution characteristic of a drunk. Jack felt a dual tinge of outrage and jealousy : outrage at the Frenchman's bill-board advertisement ; jealousy because he was returning home.

Upon arriving at Victoria Station, Jack and Alun pooled their resources and shared their combined wealth. A shilling. Six pennies each. They shook hands and parted.

Jack bought a bar of Nestlé's chocolate and a packet of five Woodbines. Without sufficient funds to purchase a railway ticket home to Abertridwr Jack bought a Paddington Station platform ticket. He'd have to " owe " the G.W.R. the money. If a guard or ticket-collector approached him on the train he'd either feign sleep or pay a visit to the W.C.

Jack selected a free compartment, closed the door and settled down to enjoy a Woodbine. Much better than the French cigarettes, he mused. A shrill whistle blew. The train belched smoke, gathered speed and left behind Paddington's pottering of porters and passengers.

Soon the compartment door opened, but instead of the railway guard that Jack feared stood the short, bespectacled Arthur Horner, President of the South Wales Miners' Federation.

" What the 'ell you doin' up 'ere, Jack ? Been to the Old Bailey again eh ? " joked Arthur, the self-styled ' incorrigible rebel.' A noted boy preacher and former student at Birmingham Baptist College, Arthur swapped the pulpit for the political hustings. During the Great War he served two years' hard labour for refusing to serve in the British forces.

" Come on, let's go and 'ave some grub," continued Horner pointing in the direction of the dining carriage.

Jack explained his predicament. He was returning home from France after an unsuccessful attempt to reach Spain. He had no money, not even a railway ticket. Arthur offered to pay for the refreshments and Jack followed to where he found the President's two travelling companions—Dai Dan Evans, a Miners' Federation Officer, and the diminutive Miss Ellen Wilkinson, the recently elected Labour M.P. and leader of the Jarrow Crusade. Jack

41

remembered her speak words as fiery as her red hair in Hyde Park after the previous November's Hunger March.

A two hundred strong contingent marched from Jarrow with a petition signed by 12,000 of its people. They hoped to draw Parliament's attention to the plight of the stricken town. This once prosperous Durham shipbuilding centre, ruined by the closure of its shipyards, became a town of idle men and machines. The town that was murdered. Ellen, who publicly admitted to loathing walking, marched with her men the three hundred miles to London. The Jarrow Crusade remains one of the most enduring images of the 1930s.

Arthur Horner introduced Jack to his two companions. The train roared on as Jack described his adventures in France. Before taking their leave in Cardiff, Arthur, Dai Dan and Ellen each gave Jack a ten-shilling note. He had more than enough to cover his fare.

April 1937.

Two months after returning home, Jack was about to leave the Workmen's Hall after a Communist Party meeting when Leo Price caught his arm, guided him to a quiet corner and whispered :

" Just a minute, Jack. Do you intend trying to get to Spain again ? "

" Yes," came the reply.

" Well," teased Leo, his face breaking into a smile, " you'd better make a better bloody job of it, this time. I'm coming with you."

Months of soul-searching were over. Spain had summoned and Leo answered the call :

" SPAIN !

We woke each morning to the thought of Spain.

> Spain in our thoughts all day
> And into each troubled night
> Disturbing thoughts
> Reproaching thoughts
> Home was no longer home
> For the battle raged at the front."

Bob Cooney.

Abertillery-born Leo was a youthful sixteen years of age during the 1921 lockout. The weather was good and Leo was glad to escape the darkness of the Cwmtillery pit. Long sunshine hours were more desirable than the dust-laden air. Leo began to ask himself certain questions. Why were so many policemen stationed to guard the pit-head ? Why did sailors march the town with fixed bayonets ? The seed began to germinate.

By the time of the 1926 Strike Leo had moved to Bedwas. Without a penny to his name, and unable to afford a place to live, he made a temporary home at the Workmen's Hall. One soup-kitchen meal a day and a bunk in the dressing rooms sprouted Leo's political seed into scarlet colour. He joined the Communist Party and played a leading role in the fight against scab-unionism at the Bedwas Colliery.

Leo began to ponder Spain. He spoke to his wife Lil about his intentions. She didn't understand. But the die was cast. Leo had made up his mind. He was going to Spain. The night before going, Leo took his young daughter Rita to bed. He tucked her in and kissed her. It was the hardest thing Leo ever had to do.

On the April morning of his second attempt to reach Spain, Jack caught the nine o'clock 'bus to Caerphilly. He had arranged to meet Leo there. But the first person he saw upon arriving was a distressed and angry Lil Price. Leo had not slept at home the previous night. Where was he ? Had he gone to Spain without telling her ? Jack denied all knowledge, knowing that Leo had spent the night with his sister Florence. He had to make the break the night before.

When he was able to rendezvous with Leo, Jack advised him to catch the Cardiff 'bus at Nantgarw Road, the second scheduled stop. Lil was on the warpath.

Leo's mind was made up. Nothing was going to prevent him from going to Spain. He had no desire for a scene with Lil on the Caerphilly streets, so he made for Nantgarw Road, walking in the shadow of the town's Norman Castle. At that particular moment Leo would have volunteered to fight singlehanded a whole company of Franco's mercenary Moorish troops. Lil would have been a more formidable opponent than the bloodthirsty " los Moros."

Jack and Leo caught the Paddington train from Cardiff and stayed in London overnight before catching the boat-train to Paris.

At the Gare du Nord station they met a courier who directed them to a red painted café on the rue D'Abervilliers. They found the café without difficulty and were shown by the concierge to an upstairs room. A dozen or so other recruits were there being interviewed by a tall, elegant woman who went by the alias, Comrade Rita. She wore a large red carnation on her coat. She was, in fact, Mrs. Charlotte Haldane, the wife of J. B. S. Haldane the eminent

Jean Winnick with Basque refugee, August 1937.

British biologist. She served as one of the Paris organisers of the International Brigade recruitment centre.

After a meal of liver sausage washed down with red wine, the group of volunteers were split up. They were directed to various hotels and tenement houses in the Combat area of Paris: a dowdy, working class locality, where the bad breath of the canals and abattoirs combined with the decaying fetor of ancient houses and dingy cafés.

Jack and Leo spent their first night in a tenement on a narrow street of high old houses. They huddled together like hags. After a second night above a workers' café the Welshmen journeyed by train to the medieval town of Arles, in south-east France.

Arles is a sun-drenched town situated on a low hill. It straddles the River Rhône and seems to spout out of the surrounding marshes.

The recruits were met at the station, escorted through the winding streets, past the Roman amphitheatre to the Town Hall, where they were billeted. Arles was the final clearing house for entry into Spain. There was a continual movement in and out of the building. Groups of thirty or so would leave for the frontier. They were replaced by fresh arrivals from Paris.

Even though the French government opposed the movement of volunteers through their country, the Arles town council and its socialist mayor Dr. Joseph Imbert turned an unofficial blind-eye to the presence of foreigners in their town.

On May-day 1937, Jack's thirty-eighth birthday, Dr. Imbert visited the volunteers in the Town Hall. Jack had expected some grand figure stooping under the weight of a magnificent chain of office. He was totally unprepared for the parchment faced, unshaven, bereted visitor who was introduced as the town's first citizen.

Dr. Imbert's story is a tragic one. After the German invasion of France he was deprived of his functions of Mayor and Chief Councillor. He established contact with other Arlesian patriots and organised the passage of information to the Allies. He continued to arrange Resistance against the German occupational forces until 1943. The Doctor was arrested by the Gestapo and incarcerated in the S.S. Dachau concentration camp near Munich. It was here that he ' disappeared ' at the age of forty-two.

The town of Arles, in order to commemorate Dr. Imbert, ' martyr de la lutte contre la barbarie nazie,' gave his name to the

The Basque refugee football team which visited Abertridwr in 1939.

new General Hospital built between 1970-72 and to the Avenue leading up to it.

May-day 1937. Dr. Imbert asked Jack to say a few words on behalf of the British contingent. Jack spoke on the importance of international working class solidarity and the evils of fascism epitomised by the bombing of Guernica a few days previously on April 26th. It was an act which shocked the conscience of the civilized world, a callous and clinical experiment in the horrors of mechanical destruction.

Guernica is an ancient town dozing in an armpit of the Basque mountains, in north Spain. This ' Holy City ' of the Basques and centre of their cultural tradition was a defenceless town far behind the front line. This appalling massacre was the first annihilation, by bombing, of an European town. Guernica came to symbolize the anti-fascist struggle.

Monday. Market day. April 26th, 1937. Guernica was overflowing with peasant farmers and traders. Ox-driven, solid wheeled Basque farmcarts were full of saleable produce and goods.

The market was at its busiest. Over ten thousand people were buying, selling and bartering.

Half past four. A single peal of the church bells warned of an impending air raid.

The population took cover where they could. Some sought shelter in doorways and cellars ; others fled out into the open fields.

For the next three and a half hours waves of German Heinkel and Junkers bombers swooped over the town dropping their cargo of incendiary bombs and high explosives.

Screaming, hysterical women clutching their children ran for safety amidst the houses and buildings which crashed to the ground on all sides. Many who sought shelter in the cellars were trapped by falling debris and roasted alive.

Fighter planes plunged low from above the centre of the town pursuing the population who fled for refuge. Insane with terror, they fled, mowed down by a machine gun shower. Even the flocks of penned sheep in the main ' plaza ' were machine gunned before the planes disappeared into the sky.

Guernica was a shambles of blazing ruins. A chaos of charred beams, twisted girders and falling buildings. Units of the fire brigade carried out what rescue work they could. Forlorn groups of inhabitants wandered the rubble in search of missing relatives.

An area of five miles around Guernica was devastated, and the 'caserios,' the isolated farmhouses surrounding the town, burned in the dusk like candles upon the altars of the hills :

> " Blossoming mornings of winter,
> Put no face to the child that sleeps.
>
> Put no features, no eye or lip,
> To the body that sleeps in frost.
>
> Don't remember the sickness of touching
> That smouldering, charred face.
>
> Or the tomb we founded for God
> On bones of vomiting gold.
>
> Strict acid light of morning,
> Put no face to the child that sleeps."
>
> *Anthony Conran.*

After Jack had finished speaking, he was approached by Wilf Winnick, a Manchester volunteer. Wilf confided that he'd been in tears during Jack's account of the Guernica tragedy. He'd been thinking of his own two children at home. In going to Spain, Wilf felt that he was fighting for the children of the world. His wife, Anne, shared that belief. Some months later, she sent Wilf a photograph of their young daughter in the arms of a Guernica refugee. On the reverse side was a message purporting to have been written by the two year old Jean :

" Dear Daddy,

I love you such a great big lot. This smile is specially for you. Can you see a bit of Mammy in me ? Dear Daddy—I am truly honestly glad about what you are doing—but I want you to my own self soon. I am so glad you love me Daddy—I will be worthy of you."

The British government was horrified by the attack on Guernica. It offered to provide ships and naval escort to carry Basque refugee children from the port-city of Bilbao.

In May 1937, four thousand Spanish waifs landed at Southampton. Fifty of them were settled in Cambria House, an old school building at Caerleon.

The Welsh people of the mining valleys took the children to their hearts. The response in the valleys to the Spanish cause was great. The generosity of communities themselves ravaged by poverty testifies to the character of their inhabitants. Spanish Aid Committees sprang up everywhere to collect food, articles of clothing and money to send to Republican Spain. (During the first week of March 1938 in a house to house collection at Abertridwr, Jack collected £7. 6s. in aid of the Spanish Fund).

After their return from Spain, Jack and Leo, amongst others, wandered Abertridwr with a wheelbarrow in a tireless search for whatever the villagers, in their sympathy, could spare. Their driving force was the memory of shortages they had seen at first hand in Spain.

They returned with each barrowful to the shop on the village square, which served as a headquarters and storehouse for Spanish Aid.

The shop had once belonged to a greengrocer-fishmonger nick-named " Sammy Apples." Sammy was a popular tradesman re-nowned for his kindness and subsequently became the subject of a number of local sagas. One tells of how a poor widow asked the price of a fish Sammy was holding by the tail. He told her. She couldn't afford it so Sammy halved the price. The fish was still beyond the widow's means.

" Look missus," coaxed Sammy, " I'll turn my back and you can pinch it."

It was with the same spirit that the people of Abertridwr turned their backs as Republican Spain pilfered their property.

In May 1939, a party of Basque children from Caerleon visited Abertridwr. They played football against a selected valley team in the Welfare Park. Abertridwr won the day by two goals to one. It was the Basque boys' fifth game in six days.

After a tea in the Pavilion, the Basque boys and girls gave a concert at the Premier Hall. They danced their Basque dances. They sang their Basque songs. They concluded the evening by sing-ing ' Cwm Rhondda ' and ' Hen Wlad fy Nhadau.' At the end of the concert, Jack thanked the children for a most entertaining evening :

> " They sing and games are played.
> Music is heard—in gala dress
> Dances are given
> Expressive of the spirit
> That once dwelt in the childrens' land.
> Teeth gleam in merry smiles,
> Eyes flash,
> Speeches are made.

We pledge ourselves once more
To fight the tyranny
Which for the moment
Is triumphant."

On May 2nd, Jack and Leo's party left Arles in a fleet of cars and taxis. They were driven through the region known as Languedoc-Roussillion, a part of ancient Gaul. This was the area of Roman buildings, medieval castles, fortified towns and antique hill villages. On they drove through Perpignan, the town of Jack's arrest and imprisonment four months earlier.

By early evening they were dropped on a quiet mountain road between Perpignan and Elne. Taking cover in a little valley which tumbled down from the road, they awaited their next contact. No-one turned up that evening.

The next night, May 3rd, the contact appeared with sacks of cheese, bread, and skins of wine.

Francisco de Goya painted the picture. Oils on a canvas, nine foot by twelve. He called it " The Third of May, 1808 : The Execution of the Defenders of Madrid."

It is a revolutionary painting, perhaps the greatest he ever painted. It reflects the political and social upheaval of May 1808, when Napoleon's army entered Spain and placed Bonaparte's brother, Joseph, on the throne. In Madrid, officers of the Spanish artillery refused to surrender their arms. The people of Madrid were quick to support their officers' lead.

Goya's picture captures the bloody suppression of the Madrid uprising. It is a splendid piece of visual journalism. The firing squad, a thin anonymous line of French soldiers, their carbines pointing death. A dark-faced man wearing a white shirt throws up his hands. Others huddle around him. They cover their eyes and clasp their hands in prayer. Their crime? Defending their city. Madrid. They were fighting a war of independence and liberty.

May 3rd 1937. A hundred and twenty nine years later Madrid was being threatened again. The Madrilenos were forced to defend themselves, to man, woman and child the barricades :

" To arms ! To arms !
With sickles, with knives,
With pitchforks, with muskets,
With teeth, with nails,

50

If there are no bullets, with stones,
If there are no rifles, with sticks,
If there are no barricades,
The bodies of our fallen comrades
Will build the first one."

Emilio Prados.

On the evening of May 3rd, Jack was on his way to defend Madrid. Stranded in a valley only kilometres from the Spanish frontier, he was waiting to participate in the crusade he hoped would liberate Spain from the fascist clouds that darkened the land.

The new contact conveyed the volunteers to the outskirts of the small cathedral town of Elne, midway between Perpignan and the frontier village of Cerbere. Elne clustered around its eleventh century cathedral. It was dusk and the street lights glowed in the growing gloom. Beneath these town walls camped the celebrated Carthaginian general Hannibal en route for Rome. When trouble developed between Carthage and Rome on account of Hannibal's expansion in Spain, Hannibal astonished the Romans with a daring manoeuvre. Starting from Spain with about 60,000 troops and fifty elephants he crossed the Pyrenees on his way to Roman Italy.

The Pyrenees. The natural physical boundary between France and the Iberian Peninsula extending from the Bay of Biscay in the North to the Mediterranean in the South. Three hundred miles of forests, soaring peaks, high valleys and deep gorges.

Jack looked up at the summit of Collado de Lli. It towered above the fifty strong group, a giant, cowled devil in the murk. The French guide issued instructions. He feared that the road-bridge which crossed the river might be guarded by a non-intervention patrol. Their route into the foothills meant climbing the adjacent railway embankment and crossing the river by means of the railway bridge.

The bridge had a walk-way of steel plates but the parapet was only a little over a yard in height. They were to crawl on all fours.

Jack and Leo were halfway across the bridge when a sound exploded in the darkness like the sudden eruption of a volcano. Hardly daring to breathe, they were paralysed with fear, petrified quadrupeds on the steel-plated walk-way. Had they been discovered? Had a non-intervention patrol fired a warning shot?

A communal sigh of relief was breathed when Jim Brewer, an Abertysswg volunteer, explained that his safety razor slipped out of his pocket and struck a steel girder below. The men hurried off the bridge into an orchard. A dog barked somewhere in the distance.

A short way into the woods the guide halted the troop. In muted tones he presented them with an ultimatum. They had a rendezvous to keep with the Spanish dawn sun and it was going to be a difficult climb. Anyone not feeling equal to the task should return to the security of the town which twinkled below like a broken diamond necklace. It was a theatrical gesture. No-one had come this far to have second thoughts. The Irish dramatist George Bernard Shaw once said that all drama is propaganda. This, then, was a propaganda for perseverance for the sake of democratic freedom in Spain.

The gentle slopes of the wooded foothills slipped away. The terrain became more arduous, rising steeply among the rocks. The troop, reversing Hannibal's steps, climbed in elephant-file along the narrow winding goat tracks. Strict silence. No lights. No cigarettes. Up through the sooty blackness. The guide set a rapid pace. They had to arrive at the summit before dawn if they were to avoid possible detection and arrest. Through the darkness, the troop followed their guide for eight hours, resting only for a brief period after each hour's trek.

The first blush of dawn saw them arrive at the summit of Collado de Lli : an exhausted group of men who limped painfully like footsore tramps.

Cairns, at regular intervals, marked the frontier between France and Spain. Jack halted, intense with excitement. In the distance he could see Republican Catalonia. His was a falcon's eye view of the fields, vineyards, ochre-red soil and dramatically wild coast of the Costa Brava. There beneath him was Spain . . . . . . Espana :
" Many have heard it on remote peninsulas,
On sleepy plains, in the aberrant fishermen's islands.
In the corrupt heart of the city,
Have heard and migrated like gulls or seeds of a flower.
They clung like burrs to the long expresses that lurch
Through unjust lands, through the night, through the alpine
They floated over the oceans ;   [tunnel ;
They walked the passes—they came to present their lives."
W. H. Auden.

The climbers scurried down the steep incline like dawn rabbits anxious to reach the safety of their Spanish burrow—the small mountain monastery of Ermita de las Salinas. The French guide who led them over the mountains shouted an ' Adieu ' and ' Bonne Chance,' and returned to the neutrality of France.

Their Spanish guide embodied a land at war. His short, stout body was bedecked with the paraphernalia of combat. Bandolier-chested, binocular-necked, and pistol-belted, a fierce dog growled at his heels.

Monks from the monastery served the weary volunteers with what must have been a gastronomic delight after their all night climb—chunks of crusty bread, sardines and bowls of hot coffee.

Jack, as he ate, watched the peeping Pyrenean sun wink at a purple-hazed Catalonia.

Chapter 4

In Training

" If I can shoot rabbits, I can shoot fascists."

Tom Thomas, Bedlinog

(Dr. Hywel Francis interview)

After a brief rest, the troop continued its descent, tumbling down the sage-smelling Spanish slopes. They reached a small ' pueblo ' snuggling into the folds of the undulating foothills. The white-limed houses, wearing their roofs like pretty red bonnets, sparkled in the early morning sun. The guide climbed upon a large rock outside the village and semaphored his message. Shortly, a convoy of five camions, covered lorries, arrived and the recruits climbed aboard. Their destination, situated on a hillock on the north-eastern outskirts of the town of Figueras, was the fortress of San Fernando.

This enormous castle is named after the King who commissioned its construction in 1753. A solid rock fortress surrounded by Pyrenean greenery, it is amongst the most beautiful in the whole of Spain.

Upon arrival, the volunteers were led to their quarters deep down in the castle fortifications. Jack was billeted in what once was the cavalry stables. More recently, the San Fernando stables were used as a gaol where hundreds of Asturian miners spent long terms of imprisonment and torture in 1934.

In October 1934, the Spanish workers, discontented with the reactionary measures of the Conservative government, went on strike. The Asturian miners in the north of Spain united to establish a separate government. They took control of the important buildings in the province. The government directed General Franco, with his

55

Foreign Legionnaires and Moorish troops, to re-conquer the province. Like a huge, quick burning fire he scorched the entire Asturias.

With a ruthless efficiency a thousand civilians were shot. Thirty thousand more were thrown into prisons. Gaols throughout the province burst to the seams as the Inquisition was exhumed from its stinking grave.

The eyes of the world watched Spain. Welsh mining communities protested their horror. The South Wales Miners' Federation Executive Council sent financial help to families affected by the repression.

Spain had sipped its first draught of civil war's bitter wine. The huge fermenting vat exploded two and a half years later. The world once again watched Spain. Welsh miners, exhausted by their all night climb, slept in the cold underground stables of San Fernando —stables which had so recently echoed with the groans of their Asturian comrades.

The morning after their arrival, the recruits were paraded outside the fortress. Run around the castle, they were told. Jack could hardly believe his ears. The castle was in the shape of an irregular pentagon with a perimeter of five kilometres. Five kilometres. That was over three miles! Many volunteers had spent the previous day soaking their blistered feet in buckets of cold water.

Anxious to rid himself of this burden, Jack set off at a trot, only to be met at the finish by the fortress commander flashing a sunny smile and shouting a hearty encouragement, "Una otra vez camarada." (One more time comrade).

On the second day, the commander devised another exercise for the men who now walked around with the stiff Pinnochioid movements of stilt walkers. They were to stage a mock invasion of San Fernando. They should advance on the castle using all available natural cover, screening themselves from the Spanish officers who manned the fortress walls. On detecting an "invader," the officers would shout and point, requiring him to lay down immobile.

No-one reached the chastity belt of the fortress walls. San Fernando's honour remained intact. Scores of supine men littered the castle approach ground like extras in an epic film production.

San Fernando provided Jack with the opportunity to reflect. At home, he'd fought with fiery words and clenched fists against an enemy he couldn't beat. Now in Spain, he would soon engage an enemy he could destroy with the weapon in his hand. It was the same foe under a different sky. Spain was the climax of his political fight. The pilgrimage was over, Jack had reached his revolutionary Mecca :

> " I came
> Crossing an Ocean
> And half a continent,
> Borders
> And mountains as high as the heavens,
> And governments who told me : NO !
> You CANNOT GO !
> I came."

Langston Hughes.

Early morning on the third day at San Fernando, the recruits were marched out of " the fortress of gold " (so called because it cost thirty million reales to build). Through the yawning streets of Figueras they marched—a fraternity of foreign workers and intellectuals. At the station a train waited.

The volunteers travelled across the province of Catalonia in a train which laboured its aged way from the green-wooded north, along the Costa Brava to the great port city of Barcelona.

Barcelona was busy fighting its own private and confused civil war. A small Marxist revolutionary party, the P.O.U.M., rejected the Popular Front alliance, and the city streets were the scenes of an open and bloody guerrilla warfare. Private armies gathered as political parties issued guns to their members. Barricades were erected, shop windows shuttered and buildings fortified. The grenade and bullet became the hard currency of the day.

The volunteers wasted no time in bickering Barcelona. All Jack saw of Spain's second largest city was an eddying mass of children selling baskets of windfall oranges on the station platform. The recruits were led in a hurried departure from one train to another. Albacete next stop.

No place could have been more appropriately named, deriving from the Moorish ' Al-Basiti ' (The Plain). The countryside remained almost exactly as Miguel de Cervantes described it in his great seventeenth century comic satire, ' Don Quixote.'

Cervantes' luckless hero was a landowner of La Mancha who sought to enliven his monotonous life by reading fictional tales about knights of old. He wished to live like them. Dressed in armour, and

57

Wilf Winnick, 1937.

tall and thin upon his scrawny horse, Don Quixote set out to seek adventure and gain fame by performing heroic deeds.

Albacete is one of the capitals of Don Quixote country. The windmills dotted here and there were hardly different from the ones the misguided landowner mistook for giants and attempted to joust. The flocks of sheep that grazed on the wide open spaces were the fleecy descendants of those he'd erroneously taken for armies and engaged in combat.

The plains of La Mancha seemed to have slept for four centuries. Albacete lay somnambulant mid-way between Madrid and the Valencian coast. An ugly town, snoozing in an almost permanent siesta, it was the administrative and market centre for La Mancha's arid wastes. Its wide central square was surrounded by drab houses, a few shops and cafés, and a handful of dusty palms, all of which seemed to have collided whilst sleepwalking and remained too dazed to move. On the outskirts of the town was the bullfighting arena and ' feria ' pavilions. The Albacete Fair held annually in early September is a great event in the life of the town. The bullfights, regional dancing displays and illuminated fair ground shine like lonely stars in an otherwise gloomy sky.

Albacete now served as the headquarters and dispersal centre of the International Brigades. Fresh volunteers were marched to the bull-ring, interviewed, registered and paraded according to national groups. Then the different ethnic groups were sent to their respective training centres.

The recruits were issued with uniforms. They exchanged their cheap suits and waistcoats for a jumble of sleeveless khaki shirts, baggy bottomed trousers, puttees, peaked caps, woollen ski-suits, bandoliers and French military helmets of First World War vintage. Jack was particularly fond of the black beret he was able to acquire—he now, at least, felt part Spanish.

From Albacete the British volunteers boarded an open camion and drove the thirty-two kilometres of dusty, unmade roads to the British Battalion Training Depot at Madrigueras.

Madrigueras is a small country village squatting on the sun-burnt Murcian plains. The flat, featureless terrain, broken only by rutted roads, sprawled to the horizon in every direction. It was here that Don Quixote rode with his dreams.

The village gave the appearance of being moored in the bobbing Murcian main. Madrigueras was a ' pueblo ' duplicated throughout

Spain: the dusty 'plaza' with its narrow exits and iron balconies below a monumental church and a single main street bordered by low stone buildings.

Its only distinction was its present status as the training centre for the British Battalion.

" Cymru am byth! No Pasaran! Welcome home boys! " came a noisy trilingual welcome.

The first sight on arrival at Madrigueras was not the looming spectre of the hidalgo Don Quixote in search of adventure with his faithful horse Rosinante.

It was 'the mad Taff,' Tom Picton, mountain fighter from Treherbert, more recently released from Perpignan Gaol. Tom, astride an undersized mule, cantered, awkward and unrhythmical, towards the new arrivals, a clenched-fist salute raised skyward.

" More fascist fighters! Hello Jack, got here before you after all."

Dismounting from the camion, Jack and Leo rested on a raised stone that appeared to be impersonating a pavement.

A young Spanish boy approached them in his ragged curiosity. Hot and dusty after the camion-ride, Leo offered the boy his water-bottle and asked him to fetch water from the well. When he returned, Leo took out his false teeth and began pouring water over them. The lad ran as though he'd seen a ghost exclaiming, " Dientes! Dientes! " in between paroxysms of laughter. Within seconds, the entire child population of Madrigueras had gathered, squawking and flapping their commotion like birds preparing for their migration. They had come to see the new 'voluntario' with the strange teeth. From these children Jack and Leo learned the story connected with the village church.

In the early days of the war the Catholic priest hid in the belfry. He began to take indiscriminate machine-gun bursts at the villagers in the 'plaza' below. Two brothers managed to climb to the belfry undetected and disarm the priest. They placed a noose around his neck and, without ceremony, catapulted him to eternity.

The children related the story as only children can. Hands waving and pointing, they revelled in the macabre details of an event beyond their comprehension.

Jim Brewer, of Abertysswg, in a letter to his parents relates the same story, minus the stuttering delirious excitement of the 'muchachos':

" Did I tell you in my last letter that we go to church twice a day ? We eat there. Last summer the chief priest fired on the people with a machine gun and killed thirty. That's the sort of atrocity you never hear of in England. The church was built in 1520 and this is the first time it's been put to decent use."

The Church became the mess-hall, the kitchen occupying the chancel area. All signs of religious ceremony were removed. Cooks replaced the clergy, cauldrons the chalice. Food tables and benches occupied the nave.

Gone the pews. Gone the congregation who once kneeled in their devotion. Gone the peasants who ransacked and burned parts of their church . . . . Gone beyond a veil of secrecy.

The parish church of San Pedro in Figueras suffered a similar fate, in July 1936, when a peasant mob broke in during Mass. They built a bonfire from prayerbooks and pews. They tossed holy images and pictures to feed the flames.

For years the peasants had become increasingly anti-clerical. At the beginning of the war, their suspicion of the Church's wealth and privilege erupted into a nihilistic anger. Throughout Spain, they burned and destroyed, ransacked and desecrated.

In Madrigueras the peasants went about their daily lives. They passed the Church many times each day. No-one mentioned what had happened there . . . . except the children. The inhabitants of the village ignored the war as though it was somebody else's problem. Silently they went about the meagreness of their daily lives.

The day dawned.

The children watered the two hundred braying mules at the well in the centre of the village. The few tradesmen opened the blinds of their ' tiendas.' Families went to work in the fields. They tilled and planted with the agricultural implements of their great-grandfathers.

The day yawned its tiredness.

They returned as silently as they went. In the evening cool, they sat in their doorways. The shabby men smoked whilst their wives and black Madonna mothers sewed. The children played.

The volunteers were billeted in a building which had once served as a cinema. On the top floor of the barracks a number of young Spanish refugees were temporarily housed. They continually played their scratched gramophone record " No Pasaran " (They shall not pass), the battle hymn of the Republic. They sang along with a tuneless gusto :

Jack and Dickie Bird the night before Villaneuva de la Canada, July 1937.

" Now we will Franco's ranks demolish,
The great Miaja leads us on,
And on our rifles depends our freedom,
No Pasaran, No Pasaran."

Downstairs were Jack, Leo and Wilf Winnick—Wilf who had been in tears at Arles, thinking about his two children in Manchester, when Jack spoke about the horror of Guernica. Now, Wilf was busy exchanging his supply of Red Cross cigarettes for chocolate, which he took upstairs to the refugees.

Wilf was brought up in the heart of the Manchester Jewish district of Cheetham Hill. He was the fourth of ten children born to an English mother and Polish father. Not wishing to be forced into the ' Rag Trade ' like the majority of Jewish youth, he sought employment with a number of engineering firms when he left school. A lack of opportunities compelled him to accept employment as a raincoat machinist. A keen sportsman, at weekends he joined the legion of young people who took to the hills surrounding Manchester. Rambling. Cycling. Camping. Escape.

Kinder Scout is the highest summit in the Peak District. Young ramblers, out one day to enjoy nature, were treated harshly by gamekeepers. Out of the incident grew the idea of a Mass Trespass over Kinder Scout. It was intended to be a protest against the enclosure of wild, uncultivated moorlands for the sporting benefit of wealthy landowners.

On April 24th, 1932, a huge crowd of nearly eight hundred gathered in the Recreation Ground at Hayfield. They were supplemented by the watchful eyes of nearly a third of the Derbyshire Police Force.

In a jubilant mood, the young people left the Ground—a long colourful serpent that snaked into the distance. Wilf was at its head.

Gamekeepers waited on the gentle approaches that led to the two thousand foot summit of Kinder Scout. One gamekeeper launched an attack on some of the ramblers. He provoked Wilf, a popular member of the Manchester Y.M.C.A. boxing team in his late teens. An all-action fighter, prepared to take a great deal of punishment, Wilf had been in too many scuffles for the gamekeeper.

The police began arresting certain individuals. Wilf fled to London and stayed with relatives for six months until the hue and cry was over.

When the Civil War broke out in Spain four years later, Wilf was a married man with two young children. In April 1937, Wilf and Anne went to see a special workers' newsreel of the bombing of Guernica. A week later Wilf was in Arles.

Madrigueras. Wilf shared chocolates and sweets amongst the Spanish Refugees as they joined in with the chorus of ' No Pasaran.'

Back home in Britain, Wilf's eldest brother Maurice, the dance band leader, was entertaining London's élite at the Mayfair Hotel with " the sweetest music this side of heaven."

A pole away, in Madrigueras, Wilf listened to Spanish children singing a noisy accompaniment to their only record :

> " And on our rifles depends our freedom,
> No Pasaran, No Pasaran."

' And on our rifles depends our freedom.' The Casa del Pueblo was a large hall which served as the political and social centre of the village. In the evenings, the volunteers gathered to hear lectures on the techniques of warfare and the use of firearms. A few rifles and machine guns were available for practical demonstration. Competitions were held in dismantling and reassembling the guns under a simulated darkness. Either blindfolded or under the cover of a blanket, the volunteers struggled with the working pieces of the guns. " No-one's going to hold a bloody candle for you, if your gun jams in a night attack ! " encouraged the instructors.

Jack soon became an adequate shot with a machine gun, but rifle-mastery presented its problems to the left-handed novice. He became the subject of much comradely ridicule as he struggled to steady the long rifle barrel. Everyone became a potential target as the rifle wagged like an admonishing index finger. Jack was teased that the Russians were manufacturing rifles specially adapted for left-handed soldiers. He should waste no time in leaving for the land of Soviet Republics.

A compromise was reached. Jack was demoted to the so-called " awkward squad," whose ranks comprised those who exhibited a complete lack of talent in the use of firearms.

Comrade Leo soon joined his Abertridwr compatriot. Fed up with weapon drilling, Leo suggested to the training officer that he would favour a more practical instruction. He was not in Spain to frighten the fascists with a fancy demonstration of his ability to present arms. He was there to shoot the buggers. Leo had talked his way into the " awkward squad."

One morning, a group of recruits was marched to a nearby

quarry for target practice. With only a single rifle between them, they lined up to take their turn at shooting in the direction of the quarry. Even Jack managed a certain degree of accuracy. His bullet thudded against the stone and rained a shower of dust to the floor.

A character named Bishop had been impatiently awaiting his turn. He was an ex-naval man, he boasted, no stranger to the finer points of markmanship. His turn came. He placed the rifle butt into his shoulder like a professional. Looking along the barrel he took aim and fired at the quarry. No thud, no stone shower—only an enraged figure on top of the quarry stuttering a barrage of insults. Next day, he was detailed to work in the cookhouse, because it was felt he could do less damage there.

There were other cuckoos in the nest. Eager, perhaps, was the strangest. The majority of recruits gathered at Madrigueras weren't practising Christians. Eager, in contrast, went nowhere without the tattered Bible he lovingly clutched in his hand. He had no need for firearms, the holy book was his only weapon. Eager completely lacked the ability to do anything practical. Even the lacing of his puttees was a major task. He wandered the streets of Madrigueras, love-stained Bible in hand. His puttee laces trailed clouds of glory behind him in the dust.

A concert was organised. Everyone was expected to mime, tell a joke or sing. An earthy and bawdy humour prevailed. Someone suggested that Eager took a turn. He made his way to the stage in his usual ponderous manner. He cleared his throat and, in a surprisingly sweet voice, sang :

" Where the sun-beams sweetly smile,
There's the land of Cherry Isle ;
There plantations fully show
All the year where cherries grow.
Cherry ripe, cherry ripe, ripe I cry . . . . . "

Eager's performance embodied the same simple goodness and naïveté that had brought him to Spain. A standing ovation was his.

Reveille was sounded at 5.30. Men struggled from their palliasses which littered the cement-covered floor. After a wash in cold water, and a breakfast of coffee and dry bread, the recruits fell in at 6.45.

They paraded on the village square. Morning drill. The political commissar's daily pep-talk. Manoeuvres.

Manoeuvres were carried out in a large wood near the village.

The men advanced over open country and through half grown wheat fields. They jumped over tree trunks and other natural obstacles, and fell flat on their faces. They learned how to fortify a position. Their lives depended on their ability to dig holes, they were told. They dug many holes.

There were the inevitable route marches, too. Carrying sticks instead of rifles, the embryonic soldiers trudged the plains of La Mancha, a calm sea of russet earth.

As they marched kilometre after endless kilometre, along tracks which became lost in the distance, they sang their socialist songs. An itinerant choir, chorusing the ' Internationale,' and ' Viva la Quince Brigada,' the brigade battle song, their favourite was their revolutionary rhapsody ' The Red Flag.'

> " Then raise the scarlet standard high !
> Within its shade we'll live or die,
> Tho' cowards flinch and traitors sneer,
> We'll keep the red flag flying here."

An army, it is said, marches on its stomach. And food in Madrigueras was plentiful.

Olive oil, for reasons of its purity and supposed health-giving qualities, is popular among the Spanish people for culinary purposes. They even have a proverb " No hay mal que el aceite no cure " (There is no ill that oil cannot cure). Jack didn't share the Spaniards' enthusiasm. He disliked the oil-saturated food almost as much as its monotony.

The main daily meal was an oily stew, a ' cocido ' consisting of onions, peppers, lentils, chickpeas and meat. The meat content varied according to the availability of chickens, goats, sheep and canned meat.

A tasteless monotony was the standard feature of Madrigueras mealtimes. One evening as the Spanish cooks were preparing to add rice to the ' cocido ' cauldrons, Leo decided that enough was enough. Variety was supposed to be the spice of life. He persuaded the cooks to allow him his rice on a separate dish. When Leo added goat's milk the Spaniards thought it a great joke. " Arroz con leche ! " (Rice with milk) they laughed, but it remains the tastiest rice pudding that Leo remembers.

Life was cheap in Madrigueras, and there wasn't much to buy except for fruit and wine. With champagne at eight pesetas a bottle and a dozen oranges for a single peseta, the recruits' allowance of six pesetas a day had very little value.

Soap was a far more valuable currency. Spanish soap was of an exceptionally poor quality and difficult to lather. British soap which arrived in parcels from home was of a superior standard and made the peasants' task of washing clothes much easier. Barriers of language and convention hindered a free social intercourse between peasants and volunteers. A bar of English soap spoke a language all its own. The peasants were materially poor but rarely did they accept the soap without cooking a ' tortilla ' for the recruits—a tasty omelette made by frying eggs and diced potatoes in olive oil.

' No hay mal que el aceite no cure.'

The hot weather came at the end of May and temperatures soared to over a hundred degrees. Some volunteers shaved their heads. Jack converted his trousers into shorts by cutting them above the knee. He wandered around shirtless for most of his time. As brown as a berry, he even began to look like a Spaniard.

During the afternoon ' siesta,' Jack, Leo and Wilf usually sun-bathed or traipsed the La Mancha plains. Once, they walked to a neighbouring village. They stopped to rest and draw water from the well. It was silent except for the hum of innumerable flies. Suddenly, an old man appeared and they were invited into a house where the village elders appeared to be holding a meeting.

In a corner of the room stood a large, enamelled, earthenware jug known locally as a ' cuervera.' It was brimful of wine with peach segments bobbing on the surface like fruity icebergs in a red sea. Ladles of wine refilled the cups many times and the afternoon ended with hand-shaking, slogan shouting, protestations of anti-fascist solidarity, clenched fist salutes and a tipsied rendering of the ' Internationale ' :

> " Now away with all your superstitions
> Servile masses, arise, arise,
> We'll change forthwith the old conditions
> And spurn the dust to win the prize."

They returned to Madrigueras in time for tea. Harry Dobson arrived on Tuesday night, June 4th, also in time for tea.

Harry, a thirty year old miner from the Rhondda, had earned himself a reputation as an anti-fascist fighter before going to Spain.

On June 11th 1936, five weeks before the outbreak of the Spanish Civil War, Thomas Patrick Moran the organiser of the

Jack, Leo Price, Frank Owen and Dickie Bird at Madrigueras, June 1937.

British Union of Fascists arrived in the Rhondda. Guarded by fourteen blackshirted henchmen, he intended to address a meeting at the De Winton Field, Tonypandy.

A crowd of over two thousand demonstrating Rhondda people saw Moran ride high on top of an armoured car. Blackshirts threw propaganda leaflets into the people's faces. Moran who regarded it as his " job to promote Fascism " tiraded against the Jews, before directing his abuse against the people of the Rhondda Valley. " Welsh," he cried, " you dirty swine."

Pandemonium broke loose. The crowd rushed at the van. The police formed a protective ring around the vehicle. Stones were thrown at the fascists. Police and demonstrators clashed. Reinforcements were sent for, the fascist van left, and order was eventually restored.

Charges were brought against thirty-six Rhondda people. Harry Dobson was one of them. They were tried at Glamorgan Assizes, Swansea, in December. Harry was sentenced to six months' hard labour after being found guilty of riot, incitement to riot and unlawful assembly.

Upon his release from Swansea Prison, Harry posed the question he'd pondered during his captivity :

" How do I get to Spain ? "

London. Paris. Marseilles. At Marseilles, Harry boarded the Spanish Republican merchant ship ' Cuidad de Barcelona ' with several hundred other volunteers.

Franco had asked Mussolini to use his fleet to strike against Republican vessels in the Mediterranean. He was concerned at the flow of men and materials from the port of Marseilles.

On May 30th the ' Cuidad de Barcelona ' was torpedoed by an Italian submarine between Murcia and Barcelona. Many volunteers were drowned including three from Britain.

Harry survived. He arrived at Madrigueras at tea-time on June 4th. The canteen stood for two minutes silence. Some, unable to control their emotion, wept.

Alun Menai Williams also arrived by sea. He and Jack met briefly at Madrigueras. After splitting with Jack in Victoria Station in February, Alun went to the Communist Party Headquarters in King Street, London, and borrowed some money. He was en route for Spain again within a week.

From Paris he went to Bordeaux and stayed with a French

family. He tried to sail in a fishing boat across the squally Bay of Biscay to the northern seaport and provincial capital of Santander. The Basque waters were being blockaded by Franco ships and nationalist gunboats chased Alun back to Bordeaux.

Twice unlucky.

Three times for a Welshman.

On his third attempt, Alun boarded a cargo ship at Marseilles and sailed, under the cover of night, to Barcelona. Because of his experience with the Royal Army Medical Corps, he was seconded to the Medical Service of the Lincoln Battalion.

John Adams, the first American President to live in the White House, played a leading role in the adoption of the Fourth of July Declaration of Independence in 1776. Commenting upon the historical document he declared, " It ought to be solemnized with pomp and parade, with shows, games, sports, guns, bells, bonfires and illuminations . . . . "

July 1st, 1937. The Albacete Bullring was packed. With three days still to go, America was celebrating its birthday early.

The Abraham-Lincoln Battalion played the British at football. Wilf Winnick boxed a big Yank in one of the boxing tournaments.

The sports meeting over, everyone settled down in the evening cool to a concert.

At half past eight, the call came. Sudden. Dramatic.

The Brigade was to move out the next afternoon. Report back to Madrigueras to prepare arms and equipment. They would be on the road for a few days before engaging the enemy.

Excitement rippled like a fat man's obesity. They were on the move. On the move, after a month's training. Off to face the combined fury of Franco's regular army, Hitler's " Condor " legion of a hundred combat aeroplanes and Mussolini's ground troops.

On the move. A ragged army of miners, intellectuals, dockers, students, factory workers and men from the dole queues.

Chapter 5

Stones Against Tanks

" They went into battle with stones against tanks."

Arthur Horner (Incorrigible Rebel)

The order had come.

Back home in Abertridwr, in the days of employment, the pit-hooter sounded. Early morning doors yawned open and a village of colliers trudged their hobnailed file to the pit.

The order had come.

And so they marched at night. Men moving into action, an army marching on its idealism. Convoys of camions and long columns of men clogged the roads.

All night they marched, surprise their trump card : surprise of a new offensive against the Nationalists on the vital Madrid Front. The Brunete offensive. Almost due west of Madrid was the tiny village of Villanueva de la Canada. Well-protected and fortified, it was an ace in Franco's defences. All night they marched holding the trump they hoped would out-rank Franco.

In the early morning pre-dawn they rested in an olive grove in the hills above Villanueva. Jack and his young Cockney friend ' Dickie ' Bird huddled together in bowel-tensed anticipation.

The Welsh contingent first met Dickie on the channel steamer. Later, in Paris and Arles, he won everybody's affection with his gregarious nature and youthful idealism. Dickie wanted to be part of the Welsh company but feared that the volunteers would be divided into groups according to nationality. Jack taught him to say that he came from Nantgarw and instructed him in local history to support the claim. Dickie learned about Nantgarw porcelain china made in a small factory alongside the Glamorgan Canal.

He learned, too, about two folk heroes of pre-first world war

71

Jack (seated left) with other Welsh International Brigaders after the Battle of Brunete, August, 1937.

Abertridwr—Mog Llywelyn and his bosom pal Ianto Traws.

One time, Mog and Ianto went on a payday spree to Cardiff. Hop-eyed and quart-bellied, they missed the last train home, so began the twelve mile trek along the Glamorgan Canal. After reaching Nantgarw they took the mountain road to Abertridwr. Nearing the top of the mountain, Ianto, complaining of fatigue, collapsed in a heap and refused to move another inch. Mog, fermenting with a beery disgust, bent down to pick up his friend and found a rope attached to Ianto's ankle.

" Duw," embellished Mog many times afterwards around the taverns, " got more brawn than brains that Ianto. Pulled a bloody barge all the way from Cardiff to Nantgarw. Too drunk to notice !"

Dickie laughed heartily at the saga and attempted to contort his Cockney tongue around the cadences of Nantgarw, Ianto Traws and the almost impossible tongue-twister, Mog Llywelyn.

Jack and Dickie waited in the olive grove. Dickie gave Jack a silver medallion he'd won as a member of the previous season's winning team in the first division of the Hammersmith District Football League. The two men were allied in their fight against fascism. Their friendship bonded them closer. The medallion was an attempt to symbolise that friendship. Both were fully aware of the day's possibilities ; if Dickie were killed, memory would not be the sole memento. Tragically, only a few hours later, the young Dickie lay dead in the corner of a foreign field :

> " A song was put upon his lips
> A sword into his hands
> And out he goes on gallant ships
> To die in foreign lands."

July 6th 1937.

Dawn smiled its eastern smile beyond the mountains. The sun rose slowly. Its rays dripped through the olive trees where the XV Brigade were being held in reserve. They watched and listened from their arboured balcony.

In the distance, down in the valley, lay Villanueva wreathed in smoke. Republican aeroplanes winked their metal at the sky. Below, black spots of infantry divisions moved forward. Shells and artillery erupted as tanks rose and fell over the crests of the golden cornfields.

Jack watched from his box-seat. Action in technicolour and stereophonic sound.

Jack (standing left) with two other volunteers (unknown) on leave in Madrid, August, 1937.

At eight o'clock the order came. Villanueva was resisting. The XV was to advance, make its way cross-country to Villanueva's right flank and cut the road to Brunete.

It was Jack's first taste of action and the bile of fear, bitter as death itself, lay upon his tongue.

Men were going into action. Trekking across flat cornfields, they were under heavy fire. There were no trees, no hedges, no cover— just bullets and the sun. Jack advanced over the uneven ground of a ploughed field, rifle at the ready. Slightly behind him on his left followed Dickie. On his right was a tall cumbersome Dane who had attached himself to the company. They were under heavy machine-gun and artillery fire from Villanueva.

Suddenly Jack heard the Dane shout in his laboured English, " Oh ma bloody leeg ! " Jack didn't turn around but continued his advance, eyes blinkered forward. They had their orders. Nothing was to hinder the advance.

" Don't stop to tend the wounded. First aiders and stretcher bearers are following behind. Go forward. Advance."

Eventually they reached an open stretch of ground in front of Villanueva. Bullets snapped around them like the barks of a rabid dog. Snipers and machine-gunners in the Church tower growled their defiance. Casualties mounted.

The company commanders met and decided that the Brigade was unable to advance any further. They deployed the main body of men into the scanty cover of the shallow ditches which ran each side of the road about three hundred metres outside Villanueva. They would wait through the afternoon's baking hours. At night-fall they would attack.

Jack, with four others, took up a position behind a mound of manure and rubbish, twenty yards in advance of the main column. From behind the midden Jack trained his eyes on the village. It was a long wait. A constant machine-gun fire issued from the church belfry. Jack lay on the dry Spanish earth throughout the afternoon's grilling heat. The sparse beards of singed-brown grass stubbles between him and the village shimmered in the incinerating light. Sweat saturated every garment. Each one clung to the body like a salty leech.

Water. Water was the worst problem. The water bottles had been sent back to be refilled ten minutes before the order to advance

Jack Roberts, Battalion Commissar, August, 1937.

came. Jack's leather tongue probed the cavity of his mouth in search of remaining spittle.

The sun's bonfire eventually burned itself out. Dusk's mantle descended. Men's eyes telescoped on Villanueva. Soon, someone would have to make a move:

> " It is night like a red flag
> drawn across the eyes,
>
> the flesh is bitterly pinned
> to desperate vigilance,
>
> the blood is stuttering with fear . . . .
> The hands melt with weakness
>
> into the gun's hot iron
> the body melts with pity,
>
> the face is braced for wounds,
> the odour and kiss of final pain."
>
> Laurie Lee.

In the semi-darkness, a group of two dozen men, women and children emerged from the village. A girl of about ten years of age led. " Camaradas! Camaradas! " they shouted and waved a white flag.

Someone in the trenches bawled, " Don't fire. There are children coming from the village." Men poured out of the cover of their trenches. Pat Murphy, an unemployed Cardiff seaman of Irish descent, hurried forward and ordered the villagers to lay down whatever arms they had in their possession. He detected in their ranks a group of Italian soldiers who were attempting a sortie.

The Republicans had fallen for an old trick—the white flag of truce as a cover for hostilities.

For a few minutes pandemonium reigned. Pat grappled with one of the Italians whilst the others fired sub-machine guns and were lobbing handgrenades in every direction. A grenade was hurled at Fred Copeman, Commander of the Battalion. It missed him but killed Tommy Gibbons, Battalion Secretary.

Copeman, his anger making him look bigger and more dangerous than ever, screamed the order, " Don't be sentimental. Stand shoulder to shoulder and shoot anything that moves."

Jack felt the alarm of anxiety ring within him. It was difficult to distinguish friend from foe in the dusk and he was in advance of the main force, behind the manure-mound. In the half-blind bed-lam, he could easily have been mistaken for one of the Italians. Jack recognised Frank King of Port Talbot as the Republicans moved forward. He wasted no time in identifying himself.

The skirmish lasted less than ten minutes. It was long enough for Pat Murphy to receive a hand grenade splinter in the groin, depriving him of his manhood. It was an eternity for the porcelain-faced girl in a bright cotton dress. She lay bleeding in the dust, chaperoned in death by an elderly woman and two old men.

Jack helped identify those of his comrades who had fallen. Amongst the human carnage he spotted the huddled figure of Lance Rogers and went to help.

Lance, the son of a Merthyr miner, so outraged at unemploy-ment in the South Wales valleys, the political scene in Europe, and the fascist bogey, turned down a scholarship to Ruskin College, Oxford, in order to join the International Brigades. He was arrested as a vagrant in Paris and imprisoned for a fortnight. On his release, Lance made for Sete, the beautiful maritime town sprawling down to the Mediterranean sea from the slopes of Mont St. Clair. He was smuggled at night in a coast-hugging fishing boat to Barcelona.

Leo, too, was baptised by fire.

During the hullabaloo of the Italian officers' sortie, Leo heard a voice cry, " Help me comrade ! " Looking around, he saw George Brown, a thirty year old volunteer from Manchester, lying in the middle of the road. Leo rushed to him and went down on his knees, abandoning his rifle by his side. George was wounded in the leg.

Glancing around, Leo saw, less than ten yards away, an Italian with rifle aimed at him. Leo stared cold death in the face and shuddered like a graveyard. The impact of the bullet in his chest spun him around. A second and third bullet grazed his ankle and thigh. With great surprise, Leo slowly realised that he was still alive. He had eluded his executioner. For George Brown there was no reprieve. Two more bullets completed the job the first had failed to do.

A Spanish first-aider helped Leo off the road and put a tem-porary field dressing on his chest wound. Nearby was a volunteer who had suffered a heart attack. Leo and he wrapped their arms around each other and, with the unsteady steps of drunken dancers in some phantasmagoric palais de danse, they stumbled to where they met a party of stretcher bearers.

Leo collapsed. His first day of action was over. So was his last.

After the capture of Villanueva, a roll-call was taken on the 'plaza' and the exhausted, bedraggled Republicans gathered to answer to their names. Nobody said very much. There was no need. The gaps in the ranks spoke volumes.

Jack turned in the darkness to someone he recognised and simply enquired, " Where's Dickie, then? "

During the day's action, Jack hadn't considered Dickie's absence as being significant. It was so easy to be separated in the pandemonium of war.

" Well, you should know," came the reply. " Dickie had it in the ploughed field the same time as the big Dane."

The news shocked Jack like a bullet ripping through his body. Dickie is dead . . . . Dickie is dead.

The bullet, apparently, went through Dickie's stomach, killing him outright, before passing behind Jack and wounding the Dane in the leg. Jack had heard the Dane shout as he fell. There wasn't a single sound, not even a whimper as Dickie died. Dickie. Young. Goodlooking. A hundredpercenter. He'd fainted in Madrigueras whilst waiting in a queue to be innoculated. He was offered whisky but refused. Leo drank it instead.

Death's masked intruder had robbed Dickie of his greatest treasure and left him slumped across the furrows of a ploughed field. The night air was his only shroud. Before coming to Spain, his only fights were in the boxing ring. No Queensberry Rules in Brunete, Dickie was knocked out in the first round. Hardly trained in the art of war, a novice in the art of life, he was ' a better target for a kiss.'

Jack felt the numbness of shock pass. It was replaced by a soursick anger. Dickie was beyond feeling, a butterfly crushed at the height of summer.

Back home in London, Miles Carpenter, Dickie's friend and fellow member of the Hammersmith Young Communist League, mourned Dickie in the ' West London Observer ' :

" With deep sorrow we have to record the death of Richard Bird who has been killed while fighting Fascism in Spain . . . . He is one of six members of the branch who felt their duty to democracy lay in them taking arms against Franco and German and Italian Fascism."

Jack (left) with two volunteers (unknown) on Benicasim beach, September 1937.

An obituary as chill as death itself. Dickie deserved better. In life and death.

It was almost midnight before the Republicans could snatch a few hours' sleep. They had been marching and fighting for twenty-four hours. Headquarters were established in one of the larger houses in smouldering Villanueva.

A guard was needed, so Jack volunteered. He needed a chance to think. It had been a bad day. Dickie gone. Old enough to be his father, he'd adopted him as a son. Jack was glad he hadn't witnessed Dickie's death. He did not know how he would have reacted. Jack stood on guard at one end of the headquarters' passageway. George MacGee, a young Liverpudlian, stood at the other. Between them, set out on trestle tables, were eggs and rice. The Battalion cooks had catered for six hundred men. For many, it was a meal they would never taste. Jack had not eaten all day. He picked at the food.

Night passed and the summer dawn blew its warm breath through the shutters. Peering into the kitchen, Jack saw a washbowl and jug of water. He decided to freshen up while he had a chance. Removing his tunic, he washed away the day's dust and sweaty fatigue. Refreshed, and dripping water, Jack looked around for a towel.

At that moment, something crashed through the window and exploded in the passageway. Jack was jolted back into the reality of war. At the far end of the passage, George was lying dazed. Officers, heavy with sleep, emerged from their quarters in bewilderment.

A sniper had bound together two handgrenades and thrown them through the window in an attempt to kill Jack. The first twenty-four hours of battle were over. Villanueva captured, Dickie dead, Leo seriously injured and Jack had only narrowly eluded the shears of Atropos.

Six hundred men attacked Villanueva the previous morning. Three hundred remained. Casualties and desertions were high. What was left of the Brigade crossed the Guadarrama river and advanced into the Sierra Guadarrama. They advanced against the vital Mosquito Crest, the dominating peak of the Heights of Romanillos. From these heights the Nationalists held Madrid in a stranglehold.

After a day's march, the Brigade reached the foot of Mosquito

O'Leary plays the jester, Benicasim, September, 1937.

Crest. Under heavy shell-fire the men advanced to within a few hundred yards of the main enemy positions. Artillery bombardment and machine-gun fire pinned the British to the ground. There was no way forward. The heat was intense. It was a day of sudden death in the sun.

Night came. The Brigade tried to make its position more secure by digging shallow trenches. All night they crouched in fear of the systematic mortar fire. The earth shook to the right. Then to the left. Somebody screamed. Delirious with fright, each man felt that the next one was meant for him.

Cramped together in the trench, Jack felt the shaking sobs of a young volunteer, his face masked in a millenium of fear. Jack whispered:

" Cry it out, boy. Don't be ashamed. We all feel like crying, only you have the honesty to show your real feelings."

Jack was, indeed, afraid. For three successive days he'd marched, climbed and fought. Sleep was a stranger. Physically, mentally and emotionally shattered, Jack dangled over the edge of a precipice on a single thread of twine. He was close to breaking point. He resigned himself to seeing Abertridwr, Margaret and Mam Jones never again.

Enemy bombardment kept the field kitchen in reserve. Food and water were in low supply. Jack decided to return down Mosquito Crest to get some water. The risk was of no consequence. He was a dead man, anyway.

Stumbling down the ridge, Jack stopped in his tracks when he saw the body of Frank Owen (Rhondda) under a tree. The sight of Frank's body shocked Jack to his senses. No campaign is won without casualities. Frank was unlucky. Jack shrugged off his despair like a leper's touch.

In Madrigueras they had their photograph taken. Dickie, Frank, Leo and Jack.

Seated in the centre, bereted, bespectacled, idealistic and young was Dickie . . . . DEAD.

Standing behind him, arms folded, white collarless shirt accentuating the tan of his body was Frank. Father of two, with a third child on the way, he had written a letter to his wife in the Rhondda valley village of Mardy. "Rest assured, I myself feel confident that I will come home sometime. I have no fear that anything is likely to happen to me." A month later . . . . DEAD.

To the right of Dickie, all khaki and puttee-proud stood Leo
.... WOUNDED IN ACTION.

To Dickie's left, buoyant and smiling, Jack rested his hand on
his young friend's chair .... LUCKY.

Four in the photograph. Two dead. One badly hurt. Jack, the
fourth, at his wit's end. But alive and lucky.

After two days on Mosquito Crest, the Brigade was relieved by
a Spanish unit. Whilst moving into a reserve position, a dozen men
were cut adrift from the main section. Night was near so they
decided to remain where they were.

Next morning, the men's faces mirrored their hunchback worry.
A runner was sent back to locate the field headquarters. Deserted.
The telephone wires were dead, cut by bombardment. The men,
collectively, decided to end their isolation and try to reunite with
their section.

Aware of a rising panic in some of the men, Jack and Morris
Davies of Treharris tried to avert the fear by taking the company on
an imaginary tour of the Wye Valley. Morris, an ex-serviceman
who had seen service in India, led the way driving the make-believe
char-à-banc. Jack, who always enjoyed telling a yarn, provided the
commentary. He described the ruined castle high above Chep-
stow's narrow streets, the Cistercian ruins at Tintern, beautiful cliffs
and hanging woods, salmon fishing, the ancient market town of
Ross, its parish church and superb spire ....

Many miles separated Brunete and Ross-on-Wye, but the ploy
worked. Minds were kept occupied. The razor edge of fear was
blunted and the magic-carpet char-à-banc returned to safety.

Jack's political pedigree, his experience as a trade-unionist and
councillor, and his quick adaptation to the Spanish situation im-
pressed the Brigade Command. He was promoted twice on the field
during the Battle of Brunete—first to the rank of section commissar,
and subsequently to that of company commissar.

A commissar was responsible for the political education, well-
being and morale of the troops. He was not merely a man of words,
though, nor a spieler or pulpiteer. He fought alongside the men
leading by example. The first to advance and the last to retreat.

The rôle played by the commissar has been compared to that of
an army chaplain and Public Relations Officer. In a Radio Four
(Wales) interview with Gerry Monté, commemorating the fortieth

anniversary of the outbreak of the Spanish War, Jack preferred to describe his rôle in the following terms :

" The function of a commissar more than anything is political .... but more like .... a miners' agent. I'm using these terms because I know what mining terms mean, and anything that the miners' agent or miners' secretary could do to make things better for the workmen, he does ..... "

The commissar was an anchor in war's emotional deluge. Idealism had led men to Spain leaving, perhaps for ever, their homes and families. Tempers frayed. Men bickered and the commissar would find himself in the rôle of a Solomon. He needed to calculate and balance the scales of his judgment.

Frequently, a similar situation demanded a different response. Jack calmed the young volunteer on Mosquito Crest with kind words. When an older, more worldly volunteer was gripped by fear's icy chill, Jack's reaction was harsher :

" Pull yourself together, you big hairy bugger. Who the hell do you think you are ? Crying is a luxury none of us can afford."

Both young and old haemorrhaged fear. Jack applied a different tourniquet to the severed arteries.

The commissar's main task was to chaperon the welfare of the men under his command ; to superintend the smallest details which contributed to their well-being and comfort.

Morale depended on so many things.

A full belly meant a fuller morale. When moving along a front with the field kitchens sometimes miles away, it was the commissar's responsibility to locate the kitchens and arrange for the men to receive their provisions.

Morale, too, was a fag behind the ear, a word of encouragement, water in the bottle, a letter from the wife. A sagging morale was always scaffolded in recognising the handwriting of a wife, parent or friend. The commissar was a postman, sorting out and delivering batches of correspondence.

Once, in the bullring at Valencia, Jack and Paddy O'Daire were sorting letters. Paddy, as ruggedly serene as the Blue Stack Mountains around his Glenties home in County Donegal, was one of the hundred and twenty seven Irish volunteers in Spain. Above the ' chiquero,' the bull-pen, where they were engaged in their task, the circular stadium with its thousands of seats tiered around them like a Roman Colosseum.

'Franco, Franco Generalissimo.' Tarazona, December, 1937.

Deserted. Strangely quiet, except for the lilt of Celtic voices as Welshman and Irishman conversed. No sound of the charge of an enraged bull. No bugle signalling the kill, the ' hour of truth.' No frenzied shouts of ' Bravo ' as the matador circled the arena to the applause and admiration of the crowd. Jack and Paddy were alone.

A certain package from amongst the hundreds caught Jack's eye. An ordinary envelope, but it contained the unmistakable rectangular shape of a packet of cigarettes. A pearl within an oyster. Real cigarettes, from back home, not the harsh Spanish cigarettes the volunteers nicknamed " mataquintos "—recruit killers. Jack read the name on the envelope. The letter was addressed to Leo Price.

Jack recalled the time he and Leo were together in an Albacete bar. Jack went to buy some drinks whilst Leo amused himself by tonking a one-fingered tune on an ancient piano whose white keys had yellowed with age. A third volunteer approached Leo and offered a packet of Spanish cigarettes if he would play some music. Mataquintos—no fear! When the offer was converted into the princely reward of a single Woodbine, Leo obliged.

A packet of Woodibnes from Lil. Leo wouldn't mind, reasoned Jack. He'd have a regular supply of Red Cross cigarettes in hospital. He didn't need these as well. Jack pocketed the Woodbines and re-sealed the envelope.

It was very hot. Summer temperatures in Valencia frequently reach over a hundred degrees in the shade. Jack and Paddy continued their work through the mid-afternoon heat. The bully sun beat down. Paddy had a canteen out of which he took an occasional appreciative swig. Jack, thirsty and Woodbine-throated, looked up from sorting the letters and asked, " Water? "

Paddy nodded in the affirmative and handed the flask to Jack. He placed it to his lips and drank in greedy gulps. The effect was shattering. Coughing and spluttering Jack piled upon Paddy every conceivable insult his mind could invent. He had given Jack a canteen of anisette, the fiery liqueur distilled from aniseed.

The Irishman's eyes betrayed an impish gleam as he insisted that he had only swigged water from the canteen. Divine retribution, he explained, for stealing Leo's cigarettes.

Valencia. The city of a hundred bell towers. The capital of Loyalist Spain. Located at the mouth of the Rio Turia and surrounded by the orange groves, rice fields and orchards of the agriculturally rich Huerta de Valencia.

Leo Price (seated) and Lance Rogers at Oriheula Hospital, September 1937.

On August 8th, Jack went to a meeting in the city addressed by Senora Dolores Gomes Ibarruri, nicknamed ' La Pasionara,' the passion-flower, because of her impassioned oratory.

Every seat in the hall was filled. Three thousand people awaited their Joan of Arc, their volcanic woman of fire and steel. She climbed on to the stage amidst rapturous applause. Jack loved her. Tall, imposing, she was dignified in that typically Spanish way. In her eyes were sympathy and compassion ; in her face a serene sadness. A sadness that seemed to tell her story.

She was the eighth child of a Basque miner whose ambition to become a teacher was thwarted by poverty. As a young girl, she married a miner and lost four of her six children in early childhood.

She was dressed in black. The Passion-flower always wore black. Her hair was black, except for a few silver threads, and was tied in a knot at the back of her head. She spoke to the people in the hall without rhetoric but with the same clarion call with which, in the early days of the war, she had proclaimed, " It is better to die on your feet than to live on your knees."

That August evening in Valencia, she courted her audience. She caressed them to orgasm. With no knowledge of Spanish, Jack was thrilled by her. Her words were Spanish, but her message was not bound within the chains of language.

In 1939, at the end of the war, ' La Pasionara ' was one of the twelve thousand Spaniards who sought refuge in the Soviet Union. In 1977, after half a lifetime's exile, she returned to her homeland, a frail white-haired grandmother. She returned to her native Gallarta in the heart of the Basque mining country. She was greeted in her own Basque tongue with the words, " Ongi etorri etxera Dolores." Welcome home Dolores. She had been out of bounds for far too long.

" Out of Bounds." An anti-public school magazine which sold alongside the " Daily Worker " on the streets of London. Giles Romilly, a nephew of Winston Churchill, was its co-fonuder. He hated Wellington College, the élite Public School for boys in Berkshire.

Giles hated Oxford, too. Despite Lincoln College's comparative smallness and friendly spirit, Giles was out of tune there. He left the campus most weekends to stay in local guest houses. He read Marx. He joined the Oxford Communist Party.

Giles arrived in Spain in December 1936 and displayed an

almost suicidal disregard for enemy fire. One morning, during the Brunete Campaign, Giles and Jack were marching together. Churchill's nephew complained that he was hungry. He had missed the field kitchen the previous evening. Jack delved into his haversack and produced a dry piece of bread. Giles ate it.

A simple incident. An act of sharing. But it brought together two men from such diverse backgrounds. They were worlds apart. Giles possessed the dexterous technique of a champion prize fighter, Jack the scarred ruggedness of a backstreet pugilist. Both men had travelled a different road. They arrived at the same destination. Both were members of the International Brigades, men described by Giles' Uncle Winston as being " the most fanatical revolutionaries in Europe." They came to Spain in spite of the British Government's policy of non-intervention. Both were adult truants, out of official bounds.

Of the many thousands of men who answered Spain's call few are remembered. Most, like last night's dream, are already forgotten.

There remains a handful whose memory will not fade. Major George Nathan is one of these. Larger than life, and as technicolour as a screen idol, Nathan dazzled his audience. Spain was infatuated by him and he became a living legend.

Towering and broadshouldered, he looked every inch of the military professional he was. Despite his working class background he became an officer in the élite Brigade of Guards. He resigned his commission after a fierce argument in the officers' mess over the inadequacy of privates' pay. Spain gave him the opportunity to become a soldier again.

The British Battalion was withdrawing to reserve positions around the village of Ibanez. It was mid-July and the Battle of Brunete was all but over. Jack boarded a camion and rode to the field kitchen to arrange food for the retreating men. The kitchen was camouflaged under some trees and mule-meat stew was boiling in the woodsmoke of huge open fires.

Men were arriving in a steady stream : soldiers, refugee peasants carrying their mattresses and cooking utensils. A fat Spaniard, wearing, of all things, a bowler hat, furiously pedalled his pushbike.

Jack, company commissar, approached Major Nathan, the officer in charge of the withdrawal. He asked that camions might

Jack returns to Abertridwr, February, 1938.

be sent back to convey the men from the front line. Jack, duty done, made for the field kitchen to wash and shave before the rush.

Major Nathan, swishing his gold-tipped swagger stick, strutted off to supervise the organisation of transport facilities.

Suddenly, Jack heard the unmistakeable drone of aeroplanes. Craning his neck to look behind, he saw three Junkers aeroplanes flying low over the breast of a nearby hill. A high-pitched whine was followed by a deafening thud and Nathan screamed, " I'm hit!" A bomb fragment tore apart his chest. Nathan, the popular major whose self-assurance bordered on arrogance, was dead. Nathan— who earlier during the offensive had calmly continued smoking his pipe, under a shady tree, whilst heavy shell fire fell within yards of him.

A rough coffin was made from trench planks. A grave was dug near the place where he fell on the banks of the Guadarrama River. A volunteer who was a stonecutter by trade chiselled an inscription on a rock. At nightfall, the Battalion paraded to bury George Nathan and hear the Brigade Commissar's tribute. A rifle salute ripped the night air as Jack, with other selected bearers, lowered the coffin to rest a few stony feet beneath the Sierra Guadarrama. Major Nathan was dead but he left behind a mythology all his own.

The Battle of Brunete dragged on for nearly a month. It was all over by the end of July. Both sides fought with a fiery determination and each claimed a victory.

" Villanueva de la Canada, Quijorna, Pardillo, Villafranca del Castillo, the Heights of Romanillos are names added to the battle honours of the Brigade. Through a month of terrific fighting, on a narrow sector in which the fascists massed the greatest concentration of aircraft and artillery ever seen in this war, the Brigade upholds its proud traditions, and adds to its glorious record."

So claimed the Republican newspaper, the " Volunteer for Liberty." The facts are less glamorous. Propaganda is dressed in opulent furs, truth in widow's weeds. The Republicans gained a very slight territorial advantage at the expense of huge losses in war equipment and manhood. Brunete was a living hell on earth. Half of the Battalion number was hunted down by the running grave of war and the plains of Brunete were littered by death's doleful chaff.

Mam Jones — a half blind town-crier.

Chapter 6

Jaws of Death

" Into the jaws of Death
Into the mouth of Hell . . . . "
Tennyson (The Charge of the Light Brigade).

After the Battle of Brunete, the Battalion was withdrawn to rest
and lick its wounds in a group of villages around Mondijar, sixty
kilometres north east of Madrid.

Madrid! Jack was granted a few days' leave in the city he had
come to defend :

" Spain, the body.
And in its centre,
Beating calmly
Its great heart, Madrid.
Weep, women, for the children have gone.
The houses have gone,
But the heart keeps beating.
Madrid! Burning by night ;
Bleeding by day
But on her feet ! "

Norman Rosten.

There is an adage amongst Madrilenos which illustrates their
love for their city :
" From Madrid to Heaven, and in Heaven a little window from
which to look at Madrid."

Jack's first view of Madrid was through the window of the
camion canvas-slit as the lorry rumbled its way along the dusty
road that ribboned across the undulating plateau. Madrid, Spain's
mountain city, gleamed like a ' live eye in the Iberian mask.'

Jack stayed in the spacious ' King Alfonso Hotel ' and spent his leave in wandering the city, visiting places associated with the Republican struggle.

He visited the grandiose and pinnacled Central Post Office, dubbed by the Madrilenos as " Nuestra Senora de las Comunicationes " because of its cathedral-like appearance. It sustained a hundred and fifty-five direct hits during the two and a half year siege of the capital. A scarred and war-acned monument to a brave people.

Jack also went to see the University City, the University of Madrid and its surrounding wooded parklands. This vast complex, started by King Alfonso XIII a decade earlier, was the scene of furious fighting the previous November, when Franco was knocking on Madrid's door.

In a confused battle, the Madrilenos resisted the Generalissimo's advance. Certain of the university buildings were held by the Nationalists, others were in the hands of the Republicans. Sandbags, desks and books barricaded doors and windows. They fought for possession of a single room or building. The squeak of chalk on a blackboard and the rustle of paper became the whine of bullets and thud of grenades. Lecture rooms became battlefields, tutorials of death. For a month in November the sword was mightier than the pen.

Partly due to its altitude, Madrid is a city of extremes in temperature. During the winter, trumpet blasts of mountain winds chill the marrow. In August it is dry and brassily hot and Jack's sightseeing was punctuated by the necessity to seek the shade of the awning-sheltered cafés.

At night, too, Jack would frequent the pavement cafés, drinking and chatting with other members of the International Brigades. There were late performances at cinemas or theatres. Madrid is a city of the night and the Madrilenos refer to themselves as ' gatos ' (cats) because of their nocturnal habits. Jack, like them, became a ' gato ' before returning to the front where he was to need every one of the cat's proverbial nine lives.

At Mondijar the Welsh members of the Battalion were visited by Arthur Horner, the President of the South Wales Miners' Federation. Jack had last seen him the previous February on the London–Cardiff express.

Jack had bought his friend Bob Preece, a fellow member of the Communist party and chairman of the Abertridwr lodge of the S.W.M.F., a present : a table centre embroidered with the hammer and sickle. Would Arthur post it to his friend upon returning to Wales ? Arthur did, with an accompanying letter :

" Jack Roberts has asked me to send the enclosed gift to you. It was purchased in Madrid where the guns are firing and bombs are falling. It is a very great compliment that in this time of great stress he should remember friends. I saw him at Battalion head-quarters. He is perfectly fit. He is not in the line or in any imme-diate danger. His regard for you is significant in the fact that he has thought of you in this period of great stress."

Jack and Bob had been friends for many years. On one occasion, their friendship landed Bob in trouble.

In 1932, Jack appeared in Caerphilly Police Court for assaulting a blackleg. He was fined £10 and given time to pay. Unfortunately, he had plenty of time but no money.

Bob Preece saw a solution. Together with Garfield Price, he went to the Labour-exchange in Park Road, Senghennydd, and pinned a notice on the door : " JACK ROBERTS DEFENCE £10 FINE FUND." They waited, with a wooden box, to collect contributions from men leaving the exchange with their unemploy-ment pay. They were observed by Sergeant David John Davies and charged with making a street collection without the permission of the Chief Constable. They pleaded not guilty but were fined ten shillings each.

All too soon the time came to leave Mondijar. The Republic was launching a diversionary offensive along the Aragon front. The Brigade had been reorganised and a number of veterans were invalided back to Britain. Others were granted an extended leave. Jack was promoted to the rank of Battalion political commissar.

Part of the journey to the new front was completed in a multi-carriaged, woodburning locomotive. Wood was being used as fuel because of Franco's blockade of the Asturian coal producing regions of northern Spain. From time to time the train had to stop to make enough steam to continue. The troops, grateful for the brief rests, escaped from the airless suffocation of the carriages into the surrounding vineyards. Shouting and laughing, they re-boarded the sighing train with bunches of plump grapes. They were heady with the wine of confidence. Morale bubbled like champagne. The levity was short-lived. Peals of laughter became tolling bells.

The nine-month inactivity on the Aragon front came to a sudden end in the last week of August. The Republican forces attacked eight fortified positions along a front consisting of wide bare valleys broken by ranges of barren hills and their snuggling towns. One of the targets was the quiet town of Quinto, guarded by the strategic fortress of Purburell Hill. The hill guarded the town like a possessive patriarch protecting his daughter's honour.

August 24th, 1937. The first day of the attack on Quinto. The British Battalion was being held in reserve in a hollow near the main road which bumped into the town. All eyes were trained across the sheep-tracked terrain to where the American, Spanish and Yugoslav Battalions were attacking Quinto's outer fortifications.

The British observed and waited. Jack watched, with increasing alarm, the huge number of casualties being carted away from the inferno of battle. Sharing Jack's concern was his military counterpart, Peter Daly. Daly, the smiling Irishman from Wexford, was a new face in the Battalion High Command. Promoted Battalion Commander on the eve of the offensive, he had risen through the ranks like a meteor.

The following morning, the British Battalion advanced to a hill from which the Americans had driven the fascists. Two hundred yards away, across the main Quinto road, rose Cerro de Purburell. The order came in the afternoon.

" Take Purburell Hill."

Spanish scouts believed Purburell to be weakly held . Three companies advanced to attack. They descended their hill, crossed the gully and began the steep upward assault on the conical Purburell. On Brigade instructions, they carried only rifles and grenades. They had no artillery support.

All hell was let loose. The fascist trenches near the summit became a continuous line of machine gun fire. Cerro de Purburell was a veritable stronghold, a barricaded acropolis, protected by nests of machine-gun and artillery emplacements, tank traps, sand bags, fenders of trip wires and barbed wire entanglements. The Spanish scouts had been misinformed, the fortifications had been constructed by German military engineers.

Peter Daly, who led the advance, was amongst the first casualties.

He was hit in the stomach by a steel tooth spat from the jaws of death.

Continued assault was rendered useless by the deadly accurate machine gun fire. The Republican troops took whatever cover they could. Next to Jack lay the Cockney Sergeant Guerin, Liaison Officer with the Spanish. His hair was wet with blood. His staring eyes bulged from their sockets in disbelief. He was the most cautious soldier Jack had met in Spain. Dead.

> " Eyes of men running, falling, screaming
> Eyes of men shouting, sweating, bleeding
> The eyes of the fearful, those of the sad
> The eyes of exhaustion, and those of the mad.
>
> Eyes of men thinking, hoping, waiting
> Eyes of men loving, cursing, hating
> The eyes of the wounded sodden in red
> The eyes of the dying and those of the dead."
>
> *(International Brigader).*

The staccato coughs of the enemy machine gun fire were claiming a mounting number of casualties. Jack ran down the rear of the Republican hill to locate a machine-gun company to cover the assault on Purburell.

In his eagerness to return with the news that he had arranged cover fire, he ran at a crouch rather than leopard-crawling on his stomach.

A machine gun rasped. A sudden shock of nausea jolted through his body. A bullet tore through Jack's right shoulder and he fell to the ground, where the glazy-eyed body of Sergeant Guerin lay swelling in the sun :

> " The eyes of the wounded sodden in red
> The eyes of the dying and those of the dead."

Spanish first-aiders were quick in reaching Jack, but he refused their offer of a stretcher. Experience had taught him that two bearers labouring with their hammocked wounded were a favourite target of enemy marksmen.

Clutching his wounded shoulder Jack made his way to the field dressing station at the rear of the hill. Inspected, cleaned and bandaged, he was bundled aboard an ambulance and conveyed to a nearby railway station.

A partially filled train of injured stood there. The flood of wounded continued through the afternoon and evening. As night drew its drapes across the carriage windows, Jack settled down to sleep. Crimson bandaged casualties lay across seats and on the floors. Blood. Wounded flesh. Antiseptic. Sweat and urine. The distinctive smells of war filled the train.

The afternoon of the following day, the locomotive, heavy with bandages and loud with groans, made steam for its journey to Benicasim.

Chapter 7

The Earthly Paradise

" In this war there are no decorations. Wounds are the only decorations and they do not award wound stripes."

Ernest Hemingway.

" And the Lord God planted a garden in Eden . . . . . . and out of the ground the Lord God made to grow every tree that is pleasant to the sight and good for food. . . . . "

The biblical earthly paradise has a replica on the Costa del Azahar, the romantically named Orange Blossom Coast that stretches from Tarragona to Valencia. Benicasim, the most attractive of the Costa del Azahar villages, lies between the Mediterranean and a backcloth of emerald green mountains. On this lushly vegetated narrow coastal plain, citrus orchards of fragrant oranges and lemons bloom all year round. Ungathered fruit lie in golden pools on the red earth. Lofty carob trees, red-flowered and glossy evergreenleafed, oleander bushes flowering in yellow clusters, fan-shaped palm leaves crowning tall columnar trunks . . . . . Benicasim grows naturally from the hills and rocks.

The Republican newspaper " Volunteer for Liberty " relates a story about the natural splendour of Benicasim.

" The beauty of Benicasim has become almost legendary among men who haven't been there. It is called the Earthly Paradise. The Earthly Paradise once ran short of bread, and a comrade of the Auto-Park at the International base was detailed to drive down with a load. The prospect went to his head like wine, and he set out immediately.

Upon his arrival, the Earthly Angels came anxiously round to collect their bread. He was as surprised as they were to find that the camion was empty. In his eagerness to start, he had forgotten to call round at the bakery for his consignment."

The whitewashed township of Benicasim was founded by the Arabs during the Muslim invasion of Spain. There followed a turbulent era as the developing Christian Kingdoms challenged Moorish domination and waged relentless war against them. Castellon was conquered from the Moslems in 1233 and from that time forth Benicasim became a coastal watchtower, a constant sentinel.

Barbary pirates, Moorish privateers operating from the North African coast, launched ferocious and vengeful attacks on the Christian coastal townships. They plundered the shores, slaughtering the Christians and razing their little white hamlets to the ground. On one occasion, about the year 1600, the population of Benicasim was wiped out almost to a man.

August 1937.

Benicasim resembled the aftermath of a Barbary raid with its bandaged wounded and crutch-hobbling halt. The Battle of Quinto had been every bit as devastating as a Moorish maraud.

It is misleading to say that there was a hospital at Benicasim. But, beautifully situated on a reflected mast of land that shimmered on the Mediterranean turquoise were a number of large villas, fashionable retreats of the business and professional people of Castellon. The villas had been requisitioned by the Republicans and converted into operating theatres, surgeries, dormitories and canteens for the wounded. Collectively, they were given the appellation, hospital.

Upon arrival at Benicasim, Jack was taken to a villa-surgery where a Czechoslovak doctor unstrapped the layers of bandage that covered his wound. The wound was inspected, cleaned and protected by two pieces of antiseptic gauze. The doctor advised Jack to expose the shoulder to as much sunshine as the wound would allow. It was a prescription for a potion radiated by the pharmacy of the sun :

" For along the strand
In bleached cotton pyjamas, on rope-soled tread,
Wander the risen-from-the-dead,
The wounded, the maimed, the halt :
Or they lay bare, their hazarded flesh to the salt
Air, the recaptured sun . . . . "

Sylvia Townsend Warner.

102

Benicasim was an unreal world, a dream, a Shangri-la nestling in the hills a few kilometres from Castellon. Remote, unperturbed and serene, the past was overwhelmed by the present. A train-ride away, beyond the mountains, men were slaughtering each other in the name of ideology. Benicasim was a world of well being and contentment, regular meals, linen sheets and pillows. Benicasim had the timeless quality of a young child's day. The sudden death of the Aragon seemed miles away, a nightmarish figment of a tormented mind.

The hands of the clock fondled time as Jack savoured each hedonist hour. It was the Penrhyndeudraeth boyhood relived. He spent long days on the white sand, swimming in the shallow water and riding the wavelets on makeshift surfboards fashioned from pieces of driftwood. They were gentle days of the kitten-sea lapping the shore.

One morning after breakfast, Jack walked along the beach in the company of Chris Smith, a Scots lad from the Lanarkshire burgh of Rutherglen. It was early and there was no-one around. Discarding their clothes they swam naked in the sea. Suddenly they heard a shout of disapproval come from where the sand merged with the low cliffs. Pelting out of the water, they collected their clothes at a canter, and dressed as they ran from the hue and cry.

The Penrhyndeudraeth boyhood relived. It could have been Jack and Twm Mawddwy playing truant on Traeth Bach. The Aragon was aeons away . . . . . . So, too, was Abertridwr.

Jack regularly wrote home to Mam Jones and his daughter, Margaret. In his letters, no matter how bad things really were, he created the impression that he was in the prime of condition. Not once did he suggest any cause for concern. Whilst in Benicasim he was able to correspond more frequently. He described how he was enjoying himself, basking in the sun, swimming and picking oranges on the Costa del Azahar. He had been granted a month's leave, he said. He forgot to mention Quinto and his shoulder-wound.

It wasn't until November, a month after he had left Benicasim, that Jack's brother-in-law, Bob Jones, read in the press that Jack had been injured.

" Councillor Wounded. Mr. John Roberts, of Abertridwr, who has been fighting in Spain, is recovering after being wounded in the shoulder, and has now left hospital. He is a member of the Caerphilly District Council."

Tom Jones was secretary of the Rhos Peace Council. He hated war with all his heart, but he hated fascism more. He was not prepared to accept peace at any price, he had watched the lights of democracy snuffed throughout Europe. He left his North Wales home of Rhosllannerchrugog and went to breathe on the flickering Spanish flame.

A member of the Anglo-American anti-tank unit, Tom was wounded in the foot during the Battle of Quinto, and now shared Jack's hospitalisation at Benicasim.

Both men were native Welsh speakers. Both were miners. Tom had even heard the name of " Jack Russia " mentioned in Rhos, a mining village with much in common with the South Wales coalfield.

Tom was wounded again a year later during the Battle of the River Ebro. He was captured by the Nationalists and imprisoned in a small annex of hell called Saragossa prison.

In November 1938, the International Brigades were withdrawn from Spain and in an emotional farewell parade at Barcelona ' La Pasionara ' told the assembled volunteers :

" Comrades of the International Brigades. Political reasons, reasons of state, the welfare of that same cause for which you offered your blood with boundless generosity, are sending you back . . . . to your own countries . . . . . You can go proudly."

Within two months nearly five thousand volunteers of twenty-nine nations left Spain. Tom remained to hear the Saragossa court sentence him to death. For three months he lived with Death's daily threat like the sword of Damocles hanging by a single hair above his head.

In March 1939, the sentence was commuted to thirty years' imprisonment, but after only twelve months in Burgos Penitentiary Tom received the news he hardly dared believe. He was to be released and sent home after the British Government agreed to a trade agreement with Franco, plus £2 million.

Llannerchrugog. Tom returned home to discover that his parents had died whilst he was in prison. They passed away believing their son to be dead. The Spanish authorities had sent Tom's death certificate. They cashed the small insurance premium they'd taken out on their son's life, but they didn't live to use it. Tom returned home to spend his own death dues.

A constant source of amusement at Benicasim was the Irish-

Canadian O'Leary. He spoke with an Irish brogue drawing out the soft vowels almost as far as his stories. Hyperbole was his next of kin.

According to his own boast he had been involved in almost every illegal and clandestine activity imaginable. During the Prohibition era of the 1920s, when the Canadian and American governments forbade the manufacture, transport and sale of alcoholic beverages, O'Leary's dubious talents were in great demand. Various underworld gangs fought for control of the bootlegging operations, and, being an unparalleled authority on guns, O'Leary's services were sought. Machine guns were his speciality.

It was a stroke of the proverbial Irish luck, therefore, when he captured a fascist machine gun during the Battle of Brunete. In his glee, O'Leary commandeered the gun and, demonstrating his skill, accidentally wounded two of his own men. In a war characterised on the Republican side by a chronic shortage of military means and specialisation, it was reassuring to have such an expert at hand !

O'Leary became a victim of his own panoply when he was wounded in the neck by a machine-gun bullet during the assault on Purburrell Hill. As irrepressible as ever he played the rôle of the Benicasim jester. Clowning and cavorting, he pulled long and hard on his cigarette, blowing out the smoke in long wisps through the unhealed wound in his neck. Only his coxcomb and motley coat were missing.

Jack recovered very quickly. He was in Benicasim for a month. His shoulder wound healed and there was a war to fight. Saragossa beckoned with its long, bony finger :

> " But narrow is this place, narrow is this space
> Of garlanded sun and leisure and colour, of return
> To life and release from living. Turn
> (Turn not !) sight inland :
> There rigid as death and unforgiving, stand
> The mountains—and close at hand."
>
> *Sylvia Townsend Warner.*

Chapter 8

Tarazona and Home

" Unthread the bold eye of rebellion
And welcome home again . . . . "
W. Shakespeare (' King John ').

After being pronounced medically fit, Jack was issued with a ' salvo conducto ' (safe conduct pass) and ordered to make his own arrangements for an immediate return to the Saragossa front.

Picking up a camion ride where he could, Jack saw again the towering Cerro de Purburell and passed through the now quiet Quinto, a dead town whose crumbling white walls and buildings resembled a brittle skeleton.

One evening, after a tiring day's travel, Jack reached a farm outbuilding just as night's quilt was being drawn over an exhausted land. Jack, wanting somewhere to shelter from the night's cold, entered through the creaking door. A musty, ammoniac smell of urine clung heavily to the air and Jack reasoned that it was a stable or cowshed. It was dark inside and Jack struck a match. Straw lay strewn across the floor and, having no blanket, Jack made himself a makeshift bed. At least he didn't have to sleep in the open air now that the nights were beginning to get cold.

The next day, Jack felt an irritation across his abdomen. He looked and saw that it was inflamed by a broken necklace of angry red beads. His head, armpits and pubic regions were full of what seemed to be large flakes of dandruff.

Lice. Jack felt a sickness in the pit of his stomach. Abertridwr had been poor, threadbare and hungry but never had it been dirty. Things were different in Spain. Lice are a by-product of war.

In the history of military operations there have been more

106

casualties from disease than from enemy action. 'The Corner of Hygiene' in the Brigade newspaper 'Volunteer for Liberty' accordingly advised :

" One of Franco's greatest allies is the louse, which can disseminate among us diseases, epidemics and death. Destroy lice with cleanliness ! Wash and clean your clothes."

It was, however, impossible in time of war to continue the personal habits which keep the body free from disease. Behind the front line it was possible to have a bath and put one's clothes through a steamer. But the lice still managed to thrive and multiply at a tremendous rate in the Spanish heat.

Jack recalled Harry Dobson of Blaenclydach, Rhondda, during the Brunete campaign. Harry, whose boyish humour never deserted him, put his hand down the front of his tunic and extracted a handful of lice from his hair-matted chest. After studying them with an expert's eye, he joked :

" Ah, yes. This one was with me in Albacete. And this little bugger I remember from Madrigueras. Better put them back, I suppose. Been butties a long time now."

By the time Jack eventually reached the Saragossa arena both sides were firmly entrenched on a stationary front. A light exchange of token fire was the only concession to hostilities and Jack settled into a boring existence of eating, sleeping and the eternal watching of No Man's Land.

Jack had forfeited his rank of Battalion Commissar when he was unable to continue his duties after being wounded on Cerro de Purburell. However, he was in Saragossa a fortnight only before being selected to attend the XV Brigade Officers' Training School at Tarazona de la Mancha. Jack's previous rank and experience made him an obvious choice for training as an officer.

The Officers' School was no military academy, no Sandhurst. Sandhurst is an institution proud of its past and traditions. Tarazona had no past—the XV Brigade Officers' Training School was a toddler learning to take its first clumsy steps.

Out of the splendid Doric front of the Old College Building at the Royal Military College of Sandhurst walked men no less distinguished than Field Marshall Haig, Mongomery of Alamein and Winston Churchill, ready to command a highly professional force of men.

Tarazona, in contrast, produced Harry Dobson, Lance Rogers and Jack Roberts. Men chosen because of their basic qualities of leadership, but, sadly, despite their training, they were no better equipped to contain Franco's threat.

The School's director and principal lecturer was the American professional soldier, Major Allan Johnson. A graduate of the United States War College General Staff School, Johnson was the highest ranking American officer to volunteer for the armed forces of the Spanish Republic. More than five thousand officers and men passed through his hands at Tarazona de la Mancha.

The pupils were willing, the teachers able, but The Officers' Training School was a poorly equipped Secondary Modern School preparing students for Advanced level examinations in less than a term.

No notebooks were available to start the course and Jack took his notes on whatever scraps of paper he could find. Later, when exercise books were produced, he copied and arranged his lecture notes into some semblance of order. It wasn't an easy task because many of them were so disjointed in their presentation—other nationalities were present at the School and often the quality of the translation of the lesson was very poor.

During the early months of 1938, Republican Spain was suffering from acute shortages of most commodities. What good then were lectures in map reading when there were few maps ; in chemical warfare in the absence of gasmasks ; in first aid if there were no bandages and aviation in a paucity of planes?

Tarazona's students matriculated in military meagreness.

Jack remained in the school for nearly two months and on January 16th, 1938, the occasion of their 'graduation' from the Training School, the new officers made their pledge :

" We, the graduates of the Second Officers' Training School, hereby pledge with all our hearts to carry high the standards of the XV Brigade of the Spanish Army ; we pledge to continue our studies in order to carry on to completion the training of our units within the Spanish Regular Army ; we pledge to carry into our work a crusading spirit for the improvement of our technique and the application of the military principles we have had the opportunity of studying . . . . "

Spain was in the middle of its most ferocious winter for many years. Ice clogged the camion-engines, vehicles became trapped in the blizzard-swept country, men who baked in the summer sun now suffered frostbite in the sub-zero temperatures.

The otherwise dreary village of Tarazona, a haggard old face in need of cosmetic surgery, concealed part of its drabness as the houses sprouted snowy-white toupees, eyebrows and beards. Children played in the snow hurling handfuls at playmates and soldiers alike. They built their snowmen :

> " Franco, Franco
> Generalissimo,
> The kids are making you
> Of effigies in snow.
> Of you, Franco,
> Generalissimo
> They're making you and mocking you
> With ordinary snow."

M. Mikenberg.

Merry Christmas ! Felices Pascuas !

It was five years since May died. The house in Church Road, Abertridwr, was decorated with trimmings and holly. A clutter of Christmas cards stood on the mantel-piece and dresser. Christmas tree lights sparkled in the front room bay window. In the small kitchen Mam Jones cooked the goose. Margaret rummaged in the pillow case that served as her Christmas stocking. It wasn't a good Christmas. No mother. Father in Spain.

In the village chapels, the children listened to the Nativity story. Mary and Joseph trekked to Bethlehem to pay their taxes. A son was born to them, Jesus. In swaddling clothes he slept in a manger. Wise men in the East saw a star and followed it to Bethlehem.

Jack had followed his revolutionary star to Spain.

" O come, all ye faithful, joyful and triumphant."

The army and villagers celebrated together. Toys and chocolates were distributed amongst the Tarazona children. Parcels arrived from home. The canteen was busy. Chickens to eat and wine to drink. A concert. Spanish comrades sang their wailing flamencos, and danced the " Jota," their traditional dance. Harry Dobson, Morris Davies and Jack sang some Welsh hymns . . . .

" O come, all ye faithful."

And so they came. Forty thousand came to serve in the International Brigades—men from all over the world, chalk and cheese ready to forfeit their lives for a common cause. Others came, too. Bedfellows just as strange.

Writers and newspapermen.

They wrote eye-witness accounts for the world to digest with its breakfast. Men like Ernest ' Papa ' Hemingway, American short-story writer and novelist, and Harold ' Kim ' Philby dualling as special correspondent of the pro-Franco ' The Times ' and agent of Soviet intelligence.

Politicians.

Labour Members of Parliament like Ellen Wilkinson and Clement Attlee visited Republican troops in their trenches and hospitals.

Students.

Young intellectuals sympathetic to the Republican cause. In the summer of 1938, a national student delegation of five visited Spain. One of them was a Tory student who climbed to the top of the greasy pole of politics—Edward Heath.

Some went to report, to write or to spy. Others went to assess. One man went to entertain.

Of all the visitors perhaps the most welcome was Paul Robeson. He arrived at the end of January, like a belated Father Christmas, with his wife Essie and Charlotte Haldane. He had already visited Republican volunteers at Barcelona, Benicasim, Madrid and Albacete " to sing with my whole heart and soul for these gallant fighters of the International Brigade."

Paul Robeson was the son of a North Carolina plantation-slave who escaped his bondage and studied to become a Presbyterian minister. Paul qualified as a lawyer in Columbia University but because of hostility against black lawyers he never practised. Instead he turned to the stage where he gained world wide fame as one of the greatest interpretive artists of his time.

The Church in Tarazona had been secularised and was used as a club and social centre for the Battalion. Over two thousand men huddled into the church to hear Paul sing. His six foot three and a half inch frame filled the stage almost as completely as his voice occupied every corner of the church. His velvet tones reached out to his audience sometimes like the rumble of thunder, others with the tenderness of forgotten whispers.

When he sang the spiritual " Sometimes I feel like a motherless child, a long way from home," Jack recalled him singing the same song some years before in a celebrity concert in Cardiff's 'Empire.' The words meant little then. Now, in Tarazona, the wistfulness of the words and melody combined with the sorrowful yearning of Robeson's portrayal seemed to rise into an expression of the universal. Jack filled with a vibrant homesickness.

"How was Mam Jones? Was she in good health? How was Margaret doing in school?"

Unknown to him, he was soon to find out.

After 'graduating' from the XV Brigade Officers' Training School, Lieutenant John Roberts was put in charge of the Tarazona Canteen. He was responsible for the canteen and its staff, the canteen-shop and attendants, bartenders and the barber who used the premises.

The canteen opened at ten in the morning and closed its shutters at ten in the night. But many were the times during Jack's short command when he opened the canteen bleary-eyed after being knocked up in the middle of his sleep by incoming camions. The rest of the night was spent in pricing and invoicing the goods.

Jack hardly had time to settle into his first command. After only a fortnight, Jack Coward of Liverpool, Major Johnson's adjutant told Jack, in his catarrhal accent so typical of the scouse, to report to the Major. Jack immediately wondered what he had done wrong, recalling his previous summons to the Major's presence . . .

Early in 1938 an attempt was made to enforce a stricter code of military discipline. There seemed to be a certain slackness, maintained the High Command. Everyone lounged around and even the sentries drooped over their muzzles like wilting flowers. Most of the troops were badly dressed in a strange assortment of clothing. They were a shabby bunch and were exhorted to improve their general appearance.

One afternoon, Jack and William 'Ginger' Bell were walking through Tarazona. Ginger was worried. If a letter from his Scottish home was overdue, Ginger began to grieve. He hadn't bothered to shave and, after a few days of worried waiting, Ginger sported a thatch of Barbarossa bristles. Before Jack and Ginger had reached the canteen, Major Johnson's adjutant, Jack Coward, caught them up and expressed his commanding officer's displeasure.

Some days later, Jack was on duty outside the canteen. He observed the elegant six foot frame of the Major stride his way. Jack, so recently out of favour, and eager to impress his Commanding Officer raised his left hand to his temple in a clenched-fist salute. The American halted and returned the military acknowledgment before informing Jack that he had saluted with his wrong hand.

Jack remained on duty for the remainder of the afternoon, greatcoat collar turned up against the cutting edge of the frigid cold. Duty finished, red-nosed and rheumy-eyed, Jack hurried into the warmth of the canteen to have a meal. The cook was stacking dishes away and seemed in no great hurry to prepare Jack's food. Deciding that no soldier could survive the abrasive cold on an empty stomach, Jack mutinously demanded food.

The cook begrudgingly provided a hot meal, but before Jack could finish eating he was summoned to Major Johnson's office. The cook had reported Jack to the Commanding Officer.

Jack left his meal à la Marie-Celeste and hurried to Johnson's headquarters. He walked down the long corridor and came to an abrupt halt in front of the Major's desk. Standing icicle-erect Jack observed the all-important military courtesy of saluting. Johnson, enthroned behind his desk like a feudal monarch ready to pronounce sentence on an erring serf, could hardly conceal the wrinkle of a smile which began to furrow his face. For the second time within a few hours he had to explain the correct procedure for saluting. The left-handed Jack had again used the incorrect hand. Major Johnson must have felt that there were better prospects for Jack in William Booth's blue-serge, evangelical army. There was no Salvation for him in Spain . . . .

Now, ordered to Command Headquarters again, Jack meditated what inefficiency was responsible this time. Johnson ordered Jack to prepare for an immediate return to Abertridwr. His three year term as a councillor for his ward was almost up, the Communist Party desired that he return home and seek re-election. The Major thanked Jack for his year's anti-fascist fight in Spain and handed him a safe conduct pass to Barcelona. Goodbye and Good luck.

Before starting his return journey, Jack went to the Battalion Post Office. He wanted to say goodbye to Leo.

After being wounded at Villanueva de la Canada, Leo was treated in a number of transit hospitals. In Madrid he learned to walk again and the chest wound began to heal. He was moved to an University hospital in Murcia. The wound re-opened exposing a large hole in Leo's chest and his left arm was practically useless.

Classed as a non-combatant, Leo was posted to work in the Tarazona Battalion Post Office.

Leo asked Jack to visit his wife Lil when he got home and assure her of his good health. A verbal assurance would mean so much to her. Letters were very much behind lately. More than a month's delay—a lot can happen in a month. The two comrades bade farewell.

In a letter dated February 25th, 1938, Leo wrote to his sister Florence :

" I expect Jack is home by now and he will have given you all the news about this part of the world."

Leo had no inkling that he, too, would soon be homeward bound, and able to give his family a first hand account of his adventures in Spain.

At the beginning of March, all Tarazona staff were gathered on the main square. The fascists had regained possession of Teruel, the cold mountain town in one of Spain's bleakest spots. A last ditch effort to stem the Aragon breakthrough was planned. All effectives were to be pitted against the onslaught. Non-combatants were to return home.

Leo packed his bags.

Jack packed his few belongings and hitched a camion ride to Albacete where he received a safe conduct pass to continue to Barcelona.

Barcelona was an unhappy city, fear was a tangible force. Bill Rust, ' Daily Worker ' correspondent, arranged for the necessary visas and railway tickets for Jack's homeward journey.

A third class ticket out of Barcelona took Jack along the deeply indented Catalan coast, pine and oak trees sweeping down to the Mediterranean. Splendidly wild and beautiful, it was not the Spain that he knew.

Jack's Spain lay in overcrowded Madrigueras. In ice-cold Tarazona. With Sergeant Guerin on Purburrell Hill. With Frank Owen on Mosquito Crest. With Dickie in a ploughed field outside Villanueva . . . .

The soaring Pyrenean peaks towered above him as Jack arrived at the Spanish frontier village of Port Bou. Less than a year ago, he'd crossed them at the dead of night. Afraid. A year. Only a year. A lifetime away.

The train rumbled through the tunnel to the French village of

Cerbere. For Jack the war was over. A tunnel ride separated war and peace. But a part of him remained in Spain with the thousands of comrades, known and unknown, dead and alive, with whom he shared a bond.

From Paris Jack sent a telegram to his daughter Margaret.

" BYDDAF ADREF YFORY." (I will be home tomorrow). Jack is coming home! The floodgates of Mam Jones' cataracted eyes burst tears of joyous relief. She spread the news around the village. A half-blind town-crier.

The following evening, overcoated and bereted, Jack returned to Church Road, Abertridwr. He returned to what he'd left. Unemployment. A seat on the Council. A daughter. A mother-in-law who'd publicly defended his every action, but who, in the cloistered privacy of her doubts, continuously asked herself, " Why did he have to go and fight in a war that isn't his own ? "

I hope Mam Jones' question is answered.

" Tell them . . . . if they ask
What brought us to these wars,
To this plateau beneath the night's
Grave manifold of stars—

It was not fraud or foolishness,
Glory, revenge, or pay :
We came because our open eyes
Could see No Other Way."

C. Day Lewis.

Epilogue

I have concluded my grandfather's story with his homecoming from Spain because that was the climax of his political expression. The Spanish Civil War elevated him to a brief ministerial position in working class politics. Had I continued the story it would have been the biography of a back bencher.

Yet, the tale is incomplete without a brief mention of the next four decades. At forty years of age, Jack was merely midway through his life.

Jack returned home to discover that he'd been returned unopposed in the Council Elections ; he continued to serve the Abertridwr ward on the District Council until 1953 and was Chairman 1946-7.

Back home Jack continued to campaign for Republican Spain as Secretary of the South Wales section of the International Brigade Association. Soon, however, Spain became a silhouette eclipsed by the imminence of a World War. Jack, who had recently returned to work at the Windsor Colliery after seven years on the dole, volunteered to fight when the apocalypse eventually came. The answer was an unequivocal NO. To the establishment he was a black sheep who had grazed in dubious political pastures. Jack contented himself by helping the war effort as a collier and lecturer in first aid and civil defence techniques.

In 1944, Jack was appointed Manager of the Abertridwr Workmen's Hall and Institute, a position he held until his retirement in 1966. He enjoyed a quiet furlough until January 1979 when he died in Caerphilly Miners' Hospital.

Jack died a Communist ; Communism to him was a credo. Over the years his faith was tried many a time, but never did it falter. It was like the church founded on a Christian rock. In fact, Jack found the reason for his Communism in the Bible ; he failed to see any contradiction between Christianity and Communism. In the year of his death he spoke these words on the B.B.C. television series " The Colliers' Crusade " :

" The Sermon on the Mount told us that we should all get a fair share . . . . . Christianity and Communism were linked up together."

These words sum up his life.

They will stand as his epitaph.